You're Having A Laugh!

You're Having A Laugh!

Martin Elbrow

Strategic Book Publishing
New York, New York

Strategic Book Publishing
An imprint of AEG Publishing Group
845 Third Avenue, 6th Floor—6016
New York, NY 10022
www.StrategicBookPublishing.com

ISBN 978-1-60860-192-9

Text Design by James Meetze
Production by Strategic Book Publishing

I would like to dedicate this book to my wife Sue, without whose patience, understanding and help during the time it took to put this piece of work together, I would never have got this far, also my agents and publishers for being supportive and having such faith in my work, and especially to my late father, whose sense of humour I thankfully seem to have inherited.

You're Having A Laugh!

The Five Important Lessons In Life

LESSON 1

A junior manager, a senior manager and their boss are on their way to a meeting. On their way through a park, they come across a magic lamp. They rub the lamp and a genie appears.

The genie says, "Normally, one is granted three wishes but as you are three, I will allow one wish each."

So the eager senior manager shouted, "I want the first wish. I want to be in the Bahamas, on a fast boat and have no worries." Pfufffff, and he was gone.

Now the junior manager could not keep quiet and shouted, "I want to be in Florida with beautiful girls, plenty of food and cocktails." Pfufffff, and he was also gone.

The boss calmly said, "I want these two idiots back in the office after lunch at 12:35 pm."

Moral of the story: Always allow the bosses to speak first.

LESSON 2

Standing in front of a shredder with a piece of paper in his hand.

"Listen," said the CEO, "this is a very sensitive and important document and my secretary has left. Can you make this thing work?"

"Certainly," said the young executive.

He turned the machine on, inserted the paper, and pressed the start button.

"Excellent, excellent!" said the CEO as his paper disappeared inside the shredder machine. "I just need one copy."

Moral of the story:
Never, never assume that your boss knows everything.

LESSON 3

An American and a Japanese were sitting on the plane on the way to L.A. when the American turned to the Japanese and asked, "What kind of -ese are you?"

The Japanese, confused, replied, "Sorry but I don't understand what you mean."

The American repeated, "What kind of -ese are you?"

Again, the Japanese was confused over the question.

The American, now irritated, then yelled, "What kind of -ese are you? Are you a Chinese, Japanese, Vietnamese!, etc... ?"

The Japanese then replied, "Oh, I am a Japanese."

A while later the Japanese turned to the American and asked what kind of "kee" was he.

The American, frustrated, yelled, "What do you mean what kind of kee am I?!"

The Japanese said, "Are you a Yankee, donkee, or monkee?"

Moral of the story:
Never insult anyone.

LESSON 4

There were these four guys, a Russian, a German, an American, and a Frenchman, who found this small genie bottle. When they rubbed the bottle, a genie appeared. Thankful that the four guys had released him out of the bottle, he said, "Next to you all are four swimming pools, I will give each of you a wish. When you run towards the pool and jump, you shout what you want the pool of water to become, your wish will then come true."

The French wanted to start. He ran towards the pool, jumped and shouted, "WINE." The pool immediately changed into a pool of wine. The Frenchman was so happy swimming and drinking from the pool.

Next is the Russian's turn. He did the same and shouted, "VODKA," and Immersed himself into a pool of vodka.

The German was next and he jumped and shouted, "BEER." He was so contented with his beer pool.

The last is the American. He was running towards the pool when suddenly he steps on a banana peel. He slipped towards the pool and shouted, "SHIT!!!!!!!"

Moral of the story: Think twice before you say something because, sometimes, accidents do happen.

LESSON 5

The organs of the body were having a meeting, trying to decide who was in charge. Each organ took a turn to speak up:

Brain: I should be in charge because I run all body functions.

Blood: I should be in charge because I circulate oxygen for the brain.

Stomach: I should be in charge because I process food to the brain.

Legs: I should be in charge because I take the brain where it wants to go.

Eyes: I should be in charge because I let the brain see where it's going.

Asshole: I should be in charge because I get rid of your waste.

All the other parts laughed so hard and this made the asshole very mad. To prove his point, the asshole immediately slammed tightly closed and stayed that way for six days, refusing to rid the body of any waste whatsoever.

Day 1: Brain got a terrible headache and cried out for relief.

Day 2: Stomach got bloated and began to ache terribly.

Day 3: Legs got cramps and became unstable.

Day 4: Eyes became watery and vision became blurred.

Day 5: Blood became toxic and poisoned the body.

Day 6 -The other organs agreed to let the asshole be in charge.

Moral of the story:
No matter who you are, or how important you think you are, you will find that it is always the asshole that is in charge.

***

THE BELLS

After Quasimodo's death, the bishop of the Cathedral of Notre Dame sent word through the streets of Paris that a new bell ringer was needed.

The bishop decided that he would conduct the interviews personally and went up into the belfry to begin the screening process.

After observing several applicants demonstrate their skill, he had decided to call it a day. Just then, an armless man approached him and announced that he was there to apply for the bell ringer's job.

The bishop was incredulous. "You have no arms!"

"No matter," said the man. "Observe!" And he began striking the bells with his face, producing a beautiful melody on the carillon. The bishop listened in astonishment; convinced he had finally found a replacement for Quasimodo. But suddenly, rushing forward to strike a bell, the armless man tripped, and plunged headlong out of the belfry window, to his death in the street below.

The stunned bishop rushed down to be at his side. When he reached the street, a crowd had gathered around the fallen figure, drawn by the beautiful music they had heard only moments before. As they silently parted to let the bishop through, one of them asked, "Bishop, who was this man?"

"I don't know his name," the bishop sadly replied, "BUT HIS FACE RINGS A BELL..."

WAIT! WAIT! There's more…

The following day, despite the sadness that weighed heavily on his heart due to the unfortunate death of the armless campanologist, the bishop continued his interviews for the bell ringer of Notre Dame.

The first man to approach him said, "Your Excellency, I am the brother of the poor armless wretch that fell to his death from this very belfry yesterday. I pray that you honor his life by allowing me to replace him in this duty."

The bishop agreed to give the man an audition, and, as the armless man's brother stopped to pick up a mallet to strike the first bell, he groaned, clutched at his chest, twirled around, and died on the spot. Two monks, hearing the bishop's cries of grief of this second tragedy, rushed up the stairs to his side.

"What has happened? Who is the man?" the first monk asked breathlessly.

"I don't know his name," sighed the distraught bishop, "but… HE'S A DEAD RINGER FOR HIS BROTHER…"

HAVING A BAD DAY?

In a hospital's Intensive Care Unit, patients always died in the same bed, on Sunday morning, at about 11:00 a.m., regardless of their medical condition.

This puzzled the doctors and some even thought it had something to do with the supernatural. No one could solve the mystery as to why the deaths occurred around 11:00 a.m. on Sunday, so a worldwide team of experts was assembled to investigate the cause of the incidents.

The next Sunday morning, a few minutes before 11:00 a.m., all of the doctors and nurses nervously waited outside the ward to see for themselves what the terrible phenomenon was all about. Some were holding wooden crosses, prayer books, and other holy objects to ward off the evil spirits.

Just when the clock struck 11:00, Pookie Johnson, the part-time Sunday sweeper, entered the ward and unplugged the life support system so he could use the vacuum cleaner.

HAVING A BAD DAY??

The average cost of rehabilitating a seal after the Exxon Valdez Oil spill in Alaska was eighty thousand dollars. At a special ceremony, two of the most expensively saved animals were being released back into the wild amid cheers and applause from onlookers.

A minute later, in full view, a killer whale ate them both.

STILL THINK YOU ARE HAVING A BAD DAY???

A woman came home to find her husband in the kitchen shaking frantically, almost in a dancing frenzy, with some kind of wire running from his waist towards the electric kettle.

Intending to jolt him away from the deadly current, she whacked him with a handy plank of wood, breaking his arm in two places.

Up to that moment, he had been happily listening to his MP3 player.

STILL THINK YOU'RE HAVING A BAD DAY????

Two animal rights' defenders were protesting the cruelty of sending pigs to a slaughterhouse in Bonn, Germany. Suddenly, all two thousand pigs broke loose and escaped through a broken fence, stampeding madly.

The two helpless protesters were trampled to death.

WHAT? STILL HAVING A BAD DAY?????

Middle East terrorist Khay Rahnajet didn't pay enough postage on a letter bomb. It came back with "Return to Sender" stamped on it.

Forgetting it was the bomb, he opened it and was blown to bits.

There now, feeling better?

A PLYMOUTH WOMAN

A young Plymouth woman was so depressed that she decided to end her life, by throwing herself into the sea.

But just before she could throw herself from the docks, a handsome young sailor stopped her.

"You have so much to live for," said the sailor. "Look, I'm off to America tomorrow and I can stow you away on my ship. I'll take care of you, bring you food everyday, and keep you happy."

With nothing to lose, combined with the fact that she had always wanted to go to America, the woman accepted.

That night the sailor brought her aboard and hid her in a lifeboat.

From then on, every night he would bring her three sandwiches and make love to her until dawn. Three weeks later she was discovered by the captain during a routine inspection.

"What are you doing here?" asked the captain.

"I have an arrangement with one of the sailors," she replied. "He brings me food and I get a free trip to America. Plus he's screwing me."

"He certainly is," replied the captain.

"This is the Torpoint Ferry."

EXTRACTS FROM BRITISH NEWSPAPERS

1) Commenting on a complaint from a Mr. Arthur Purdey about a large gas bill, a spokesman for North West Gas said, "We agree it was rather high for the time of the year. It's possible Mr. Purdey has been charged for the gas used up during the explosion that destroyed his house."

2) Police reveal that a woman arrested for shoplifting had a whole salami in her underwear. When asked why, she said it was because she was missing her Italian boyfriend.

3) Irish police are being handicapped in a search for a stolen van, because they cannot issue a description. It's a Special Branch vehicle and they don't want the public to know what it looks like.

4) A young girl who was blown out to sea on a set of inflatable teeth was rescued by a man on an inflatable lobster. A coast guard spokesman commented, "This sort of thing is all too common."

5) At the height of the gale, the harbor master radioed a coastguard and asked him to estimate the wind speed. He replied he was sorry, but he didn't have a gauge. However, if it was any help, the wind had just blown his Land Rover off the cliff.

6) Mrs. Irene Graham of Thorpe Avenue, Boscombe, delighted the audience with her reminiscence of the German prisoner of war who was sent each week to do her garden. He was repatriated at the end of 1945, she recalled.

"He'd always seemed a nice friendly chap, but when the crocuses came up in the middle of our lawn in February 1946, they spelt out 'Heil Hitler.' "

LONDON TUBE

Below is a list of actual announcements that London Tube train drivers have made to their passengers:

1) "Ladies and Gentlemen, I do apologize for the delay to your service. I know you're all dying to get home, unless, of course, you happen to be married to my ex-wife, in which case you'll want to cross over to the Westbound and go in the opposite direction."

2) "Your delay this evening is caused by the line controller suffering from E & B syndrome: not knowing his elbow from his backside. I'll let you know any further information as soon as I'm given any."

3) "Do you want the good news first or the bad news? The good news is that last Friday was my birthday and I hit the town and had a great time. The bad news is that there is a points failure somewhere between Stratford and East Ham, which means we probably won't reach our destination."

4) "Ladies and gentlemen, we apologize for the delay, but there is a security alert at Victoria station and we are therefore stuck here for the foreseeable future, so let's take our minds off it and pass some time together. All together now...'Ten green bottles, hanging on a wall...'"

5) "We are now travelling through Baker Street...As you can see, Baker Street is closed. It would have been nice if they had actually told me, so I could tell you earlier, but no, they don't think about things like that."

6) "Beggars are operating on this train. Please do NOT encourage these professional beggars. If you have any spare change, please give it to a registered charity. Failing that, give it to me."

7) During an extremely hot rush hour on the Central Line, the driver announced in a West Indian drawl: "Step right this way for the sauna, ladies and gentleman... unfortunately, towels are not provided."

8) "Let the passengers off the train FIRST!" (Pause) "Oh go on then, stuff yourselves in like sardines, see if I care—I'm going home..."

9) "Please allow the doors to close. Try not to confuse this with 'Please hold the doors open.' The two are distinct and separate instructions."

10) "Please note that the beeping noise coming from the doors means that the doors are about to close. It does not mean throw yourself or your bags into the doors."

11) "We can't move off because some idiot has their hand stuck in the door."

12) "To the gentleman wearing the long grey coat trying to get on the second carriage—what part of 'stand clear of the doors' don't you understand?"

13) "Please move all baggage away from the doors." (Pause...)

"Please move ALL belongings away from the doors." (Pause...)

"This is a personal message to the man in the brown suit wearing glasses at the rear of the train: Put the pie down,

Four-eyes, and move your bloody golf clubs away from the door before I come down there and shove them up your arse sideways!"

14) "May I remind all passengers that there is strictly no smoking allowed on any part of the Underground. However, if you are smoking a joint, it's only fair that you pass it round the rest of the carriage."

THE ONION AND THE CHRISTMAS TREE

The family is sitting at the dinner table. The son asks his father, "Dad, how many kinds of boobies are there?"

The father, surprised, answers, "Well, son, there's three kinds of breasts. In her twenties a woman's breasts are like melons, round and firm. In her thirties and forties, they are like pears, still nice, but hanging a bit. After fifty, they are like onions."

"ONIONS?"

"Yes, you see them, and they make you cry!"

This infuriated his wife and daughter, so the daughter says, "Mum, how many types of willies are there?"

The mother, surprised, smiles and answers, "Well, dear, a man goes through three phases. In his twenties, his willy is like an oak tree, mighty and hard. In his thirties and forties, it is like a birch tree, flexible but reliable. After his fifties, it is like a Christmas tree."

"A Christmas tree?"

"Yes, dear, dead from the root up and the balls are for decoration only!"

Merry Christmas!

THE BLIND MAN

While redecorating a church, three nuns become extremely hot and sweaty in their habits, so Mother Superior says, "Let's take our clothes off, and work naked."

The other two nuns disapprove, and ask, "What if someone sees us?"

But the Mother Superior says, "Don't worry, no one will see us, we'll just lock the door."

So the other nuns agree, strip down, and return to work. Suddenly, they hear a knock at the door, and grab their clothes in a panic. Mother Superior runs to the door and calls through, "Who is it?"

"Blind man," a man's voice comes back. So she opens the door and lets in the blind man, who turns to the nuns and says, "Great tits, ladies, now where do you want these blinds?"

THE FINAL COUNTDOWN

After undergoing a full medical, a nervous man summons up the courage to ask his doctor: "How long have I got left to live?"

"Okay, I'll give it to you straight," the doctor replies. "Ten…"

"Ten what?" asks the terrified man. "Years, months, weeks, days?"

"Ten, nine, eight…"

JOKE SIGNS

Sign on the door of a vet's waiting room: "Back in five minutes. Sit... Stay!"

A sign over a gynaecologist's office: "Dr. Jones, at your cervix."

On the door of a plastic surgeon's office: "We can help you pick your nose!"

At an optometrist's office: "If you don't see what you're looking for, you've come to the right place."

On a maternity room door: "Push. Push. PUUUSSSSHHHH!!!!!"

In the front yard of a funeral home: "Drive carefully. We'll wait."

In the non-smoking area of a restaurant: "If we see smoke, we will assume you are on fire and take appropriate action."

Outside a muffler shop: "No appointment necessary. We hear you coming."

An ad on the side of a plumber's van: "We repair what your husband fixed"

Another slogan on the van of a plumbing company: "Don't sleep with a drip. Call your plumber."

On an electrician's van: "Let us remove your shorts."

Pizza shop slogan: "Seven days without pizza makes one weak."

Two cows standing next to each other in a field. Daisy says to Dolly, "I was artificially inseminated this morning."

"I don't believe you," replies Dolly.

"It's true, no bull!"

***

A university student delivers a pizza to an old man's house. "I suppose you want a tip?" says the old man.

"That would be great," says the student, "but the other guy who does deliveries told me not to expect too much – he said if I got 50p, I'd be lucky."

The old man looks hurt. "Well, to prove him wrong, here's £5. What are you studying?"
"Applied psychology," replies the student.

***

A BLONDE'S DREAM

A blonde keeps having the same weird dream, so she goes to her doctor.

Doctor: "What is your dream about?"

Blonde: "I am being chased by a vampire..."

Doctor: "So, where are you in this dream?"

Blonde: "I am running in a hallway."

Doctor: "Then what happens?"

Blonde: "Well, that's the weird thing. In every single dream, the same thing happens. I always come to a door, but I can't open it. I keep pushing the door and pushing the door, but it won't budge!"

Doctor: "Does the door have any letters on it?"

Blonde: "Yes."

Doctor: "And what do these letters spell?"

Blonde: "P... U... L... L..."

***

PLANE STUPID

The Pope, a schoolboy, and an unnamed American President are in a plane. Suddenly the pilot suffers a heart attack and the craft takes a nosedive. As the engines sputter, the three passengers try to stay calm.

"Well," says the Pope, "we have established that none of us can land this baby, so we're going to have to jump for it."

"But there are only two parachutes," says the boy, pointing to a pile of bundles by the exit.

Without hesitating, the American President rushes over to them, takes one, and shouts, "I am the President of the United States of America. I am the world's most powerful leader. And apart from that, I am the most intelligent President in the history of my country. I have a responsibility to my people not to die."

With that, he leaps out of the plane.

Now the Pope turns calmly to the schoolboy and says: "I am already old. I have already lived my life as a good person and a priest. There is a place for me in heaven. I insist you take the last parachute."

"No need," says the boy, "America's most intelligent President has taken my schoolbag…"

***

Ex England football Manager, Steve McLaren decided he was going to go to the F.A. ball dressed as a pumpkin.

He was hoping somebody would be able to turn him into a coach.

***

Poor Dai Jones was lying in bed with not much longer to live, when he detected in the air, the aroma of his wife's home baking, and yes, it was his favourite, welsh scones.

So Dai thought, *it's no good, before I die, I must just have one last taste of my favorite scone.*

Having managed to get out of bed and crawl downstairs, he made his way to the kitchen on his hands and knees.

He approached the table gasping for breath and reached up to take a scone.

He was just about to take one of his wife's desired scones from the plate when a rolling pin rattled across his knuckles and his wife exclaimed in a high pitched scream: "Oh no you don't, Dai Jones. These are for your funeral!"

***

A man walks into his Doctor's surgery and says, "Doc, I think I have broken my arm."

The Doctor examines the man's arm and says, "You're correct, it is broken."

To which the man asks, "Will I be able to play the piano when it's mended?"

The Doctor replies, "Of course you will."

The man says, "That's funny, I couldn't before!"

***

Jack was lying in bed waiting for the moment when his life would end.

At his bedside, holding his hand was his devoted wife.

His eyes flickered open. He looked up at his wife and said, "There is something I must tell you."

"Hush," whispered his wife, "you must rest."

"No, no, I must tell you," Jack said, "I have a confession to make, for I have slept with your mother, your sister, your sister's best friend and your best friend Janet!"

"I know," whispered his wife softly, "now just lay back and let the poison do its work!"

***

Yes, it's Saturday night and it's time for everybody's favourite TV show: Stars in Their Eyes.

The first act finished and Matthew Kelly started to introduce the next contestant. "And now, ladies and gentlemen, our next act is going to be performed by a very brave man, please give a very warm welcome to Simon."

Simon walks onto the stage and shakes hands with Matthew Kelly, who says, "Simon, before you tell us who you are going to be tonight, briefly explain the recent trauma that you have experienced."

"Well, Matthew," said Simon, "my Uncle Ted and I were driving up the motorway when we were involved in the most horrific car crash. Unfortunately my Uncle did not survive and I had my left arm and leg torn off."

"Wow," said Matthew Kelly, "yet you look great tonight, how come?"

"I was extremely lucky Matthew, although my uncle died in the accident, the surgeons were able to use his limbs to replace those that I had lost."

"Okay, Simon, you are a brave man, please, tell us who you are going to be?"

"Tonight, Matthew, I am going to be none other than Simon and Arfuncle!"

***

There was this family of three balloons, Daddy balloon, Mummy balloon and Baby balloon.

One morning, Baby balloon got into bed with Mummy and Daddy balloon and started playing with Daddy balloon's knot, to which he was told to stop and go to sleep. So he turned over and started playing with the knot on Mummy balloon, who said, "stop playing with my knot and go to sleep!"

This wasn't good enough for Baby balloon who climbed out of bed and went downstairs. When Mummy and Daddy balloon awoke, they went downstairs, only to find Baby balloon sitting in a chair playing with his own knot.

"Stop this at once," said Daddy balloon, "you should be ashamed of yourself, not only have you let yourself down, but you also let your Mother down and you have let me down!"

***

A man gets home early from work one day to find his wife wearing nothing but a very sexy negligee.

The wife says to her husband, "Tie me up and do whatever you want."

So he tied her up and went and played a round of golf.

***

A Father asked his ten-year-old son if he knew about the birds and the bees.

"I don't want to know!" the child said, bursting into tears. "Promise me you won't tell me."

Confused, the father asked what was wrong.

"Oh, Dad," the boy sobbed, "when I was six I got the no Santa speech. At seven, I got the there's no Easter bunny speech. When I was eight, you hit me with the there's no Tooth Fairy speech. If you tell me that grown-ups don't really shag, I'll have nothing left to live for."

***

One morning while making breakfast, a man walked up to his wife, pinched her on the butt and said, "If you firmed this up, we could get rid of your control top pantyhose."

While this was on the edge of intolerable, she kept silent.

The next morning, the man woke his wife with a pinch on each of her breasts and said, "You know, if you firmed these up, we could get rid of your bra."

This was beyond a silent response, so she rolled over and grabbed him by his dangler. With a death grip in place, she said, "You know, if you firmed this up, we could get rid of the gardener, the postman, the pool man and your brother!"

***

"My dog's got no nose!"

"How does he smell?"

"Awful!"

***

"Our dog is very talented, he's musical!"

"Musical?"

"Yes, he hums in the hot weather."

***

"Knock, Knock!"

"Who's there?"

"The Doctor!"

"Doctor Who?"

***

Question: "What do call a chicken in a shell suit?"

Answer: "An egg!"

***

Question: "What do you get if you cross a football club with a tub of ice cream?"

Answer: "Aston Vanilla!"

***

Question: "How does Santa take his photos?"

Answer: "With his North Pole-aroid!"

***

Question: "What has a bed but does not sleep and a mouth but does not speak?"

Answer: "A river!"

***

Question: "What did the beaver say to the tree?"

Answer: "Nice gnawing you!"

***

A BLONDE'S BRAIN AT WORK

A blonde, a brunette, and a redhead all work at the same office for a female boss who always goes home early.

"Hey, girls," says the brunette one day, "let's go home early tomorrow. She'll never know."

So the next day, they all leave right after the boss does. The brunette gets some extra gardening done, the redhead goes to a bar, and the blonde goes home to find her husband having sex with the female boss.

She quietly sneaks out of the house and vows to return home at her normal time the next day.

In the morning, the brunette says: "That was fun, we should do it again sometime."

"No way," says the blonde. "I almost got caught!"

A BLONDE'S ACCESORIES

Question: "What does a blonde put behind her ears to make her more attractive?"

Answer: "Her ankles!"

CAR-CROSSED LOVERS

A woman and a man driver are involved in a horrific collision, but amazingly both escape completely unhurt, although their cars are written off.

As they crawl out of the wreckage, the man sees the woman is blonde and strikingly beautiful.

The woman turns to the man and gushes breathlessly: "That's incredible—both our cars are demolished but we're fine. It must be a sign from God that we are meant to be together!"

Sensing a promise, the man stammers back, "Oh yes, I agree with you completely!"

She goes on, "And look! Though my car was destroyed, this bottle of wine survived intact, too! It must be another sign. Let's drink to our love!"

"Well, okay!" says the man, going with the moment. She offers him the bottle, which he readily accepts, downs half of it and hands it back.

"Your turn," says the man.

"No, thanks," says the woman, "I think I'll just wait for the police."

CHRISTMAS BONUS

Three dustmen are doing their last round before Christmas. The first goes to a house, knocks, and finds himself being invited in by a stunning blonde, who takes him upstairs and gives him a good seeing to.

Afterwards, he rushes out and brags to his two pals about it. So the second decides to try his luck. Sure enough, the same thing happens to him.

Finally, the dustcart driver, reckoning he's on to a sure thing, gets out and knocks on the door.

The woman answers, smiles and gives him a fiver.

Severely disappointed, the man asks: "How come I just get money, when you gave my pals a proper Christmas bonus?"

"Well," the woman replies, "when I asked my husband about tipping you all, he said, 'Give the driver £5—screw the other two.'"

PILLOW TALK

Question: "What do blondes say after sex?"

Answer 1: "Thanks, guys."

Answer 2: "Are you boys all in the same band?"

SPOT THE DIFFERENCE

Question: "What's the difference between OJ Simpson and the England football team?"

Answer: "OJ Simpson had a more credible defense."

DELUSIONS OF GRANDEUR

Ronaldo, Luis Figo, and Wayne Rooney are standing before God at the throne of Heaven. God looks at them and says, "Before granting you a place at my side, I must first ask you what you believe in."

Addressing Ronaldo first, he asks, "What do you believe in?"

Ronaldo looks God in the eye and states passionately, "I believe football to be the food of life. Nothing else brings such joy to so many people – from the slums of Rio to the bright lights of Madrid. I devoted my life to bringing such joy to people who stood on the terraces supporting their club."

God looks up and offers Ronaldo the seat to his left.

Gods then turns to Luis Figo: "And you, Luis, tell me, what do you believe in?"

Figo stands tall and proud. "I believe courage, honor, and passion are the fundamentals of life; I've spent my whole playing career providing a living embodiment of these traits."

God, moved by the passion of the speech, offers Figo the seat to his right. Finally he turns to Wayne Rooney, "And you, Wayne, what do you believe in?"

"I believe," says Rooney, "you're sitting in my seat."

BEING A RED

A primary school teacher starts a new job on Merseyside. Hoping to make a good impression, she tells her class she is a Liverpool fan and asks the students to raise their hands if they too support the Reds. Everyone raises his or her hand apart from one girl. The teacher looks at the girl with surprise and says, "Let me guess, Mary, you support Everton, right?"

"Nope, I support Manchester United," Mary replies.

The teacher can't believe her ears. "Mary, why are you a United fan?"

"Because my Mum and Dad are from Manchester, and they both support United."

"Well," says the teacher. "That's no reason for you to be a United fan. You don't have to copy your parents. What if your mother was a prostitute, and your father was a drug addict, what would you be then?"

"I'd be a Liverpool fan."

THE GREAT ROBBERY

A burglary recently took place at the ground of Newcastle United football club, of which, the entire contents of the trophy room were stolen. The police are said to be looking for a man who got away with a black-and-white carpet.

ROUND THE BEND

A man is speeding down a narrow mountain road, when a woman comes hurtling round the corner. He swerves to avoid her, but as she passes she leans out the window and screams, "PIG!" Astonished, the man turns and yells back, "BITCH!" as he reaches the bend and crashes into a pig.

THREE BLIND DRUNK MICE

Three macho mice are sitting at a bar discussing just how tough they were.

The first mouse slams a shot and says, "I play with mouse traps for fun. I'll run into one on purpose and as it is closing on me, I grab the bar and bench press it twenty to thirty times." And, with that, he slams another shot.

The second mouse slams a shot and says, "That's nothing. I take those poison bait tablets, cut them up, and snort them, just for the fun of it." And, with that, he slams another shot.

The third mouse slams a shot, gets up, and turns to walk away.

"Where the hell do you think you're going?" asked his friends.

The third mouse stops and replies, "I'm going home to shag the cat."

MUCKY DUCK

A woman is taking a stroll through the woods, when a little white duck, covered in filth, crosses her path.

"Let me clean you," the woman says, taking a tissue from her purse.

The woman walks on a little further and encounters another duck, also with muck all over it. Again, she produces a tissue and cleans the bird. Afterwards, she hears a voice from the bushes.

"Excuse me, madam," it says. "Do you have any more tissues?"

"No, I'm afraid I've run out," the woman replies.

"All right," the voice says. "I'll just have to use another duck then."

THE TURKEY AND THE BULL

A turkey is chatting with a bull.

"I would love to be able to get to the top of that tree," sighs the turkey, "but I just haven't got the energy."

"Well, why don't you nibble on some of my droppings?" replies the bull. "They're packed with nutrients."

The turkey pecks at a lump of dung and finds that it actually gives him enough strength to reach the first branch of the tree.

The next day, after eating some more dung, he reaches the second branch.

Finally after a week, there he is proudly perched at the top of the tree.

Unfortunately he is spotted by a farmer, who shoots him out of the tree.

Moral of the story: Bullshit might get you to the top, but it won't keep you there.

THE CHICKEN AND THE HORSE

A horse and a chicken are playing in a meadow. Suddenly the horse falls into a mud hole and starts sinking. He tells the chicken to go and get the farmer to help pull him out to safety. The chicken runs to the farmer, but the farmer can't be found. So he drives the farmer's Mercedes back to the hole and ties some rope around the bumper. He then throws the other end of the rope to his friend and drives forward saving the horse from sinking.

A few days later, the chicken and horse are playing in the meadow again, and the chicken falls into a mud hole. The chicken tells the horse to go and get some help from the farmer. The horse says: "I think I can get you out."

So he stretches over the width of the hole and says: "Grab hold of my 'thing' and pull yourself up."

The chicken does this and is pulled to safety.

Moral of the story: If you are hung like a horse, you don't need a Mercedes to pick up chicks.

THE PRAWN AND THE COD

One day, in the shark-infested waters of the Caribbean, two prawns called Justin and Christian are discussing the pressures of being a preyed upon prawn.

"I hate being a prawn," says Justin. "I wish I were a shark."

Suddenly, a mysterious cod appears. "Your wish is granted," he says.

Instantly, Justin becomes a shark. Horrified, Christian swims away, afraid his former friend might eat him. As time passes, Christian continues to avoid Justin, leaving the shrimp-turned-man-eater lonely and frustrated. So when he bumps into the cod again, he begs the mysterious fish to change him back. Lo and behold, Justin is turned back into a prawn. With tears of joy in his tiny little eyes, he swims back to the reef to seek out Christian.

As he approaches, he shouts out, "It's me, Justin, your old friend. I've changed.... I've found Cod. I'm a prawn again, Christian."

STRAIGHT-TALKING BIRDS

A woman approaches her priest and tells him, "Father, I have a problem. I have two female talking parrots, but they only know how to say one thing."

"What do they say?" the priest inquires.

"They only know how to say, 'Hi, we're prostitutes. Want to have some fun?'"

"That's terrible!" the priest exclaims. "But I have a solution to your problem. Bring your two female parrots over to my house and I will put them with my two male parrots, whom I have taught to pray and read the Bible. My parrots will teach your parrots to stop saying that terrible phrase and your female parrots will learn to praise and worship."

"Thank you!" the woman exclaims.

The next day the woman brings her female parrots to the priest's house. His two male parrots are holding beads and praying.

When the lady puts her two female parrots, in the cage with the two male parrots, she hears the two say, "Hi! We're prostitutes. Want to have some fun?"

At which one male parrot looks at the other and shouts, "Put the beads away! Our prayers have been answered!"

BOOBY TRAP

Question: "Why are women's breasts like a train set a kid gets at Christmas time?"

Answer: "Because they were originally made for children but the father wants to play with them!"

CHRISTMAS SICKIE

Question: "What do you get if you eat the Christmas decorations?"

Answer: "Tinsellitis!"

SOLO SANTA

Question: "Why doesn't Santa have any children?"

Answer: "Because he only comes once a year, and when he does, it's down the chimney!"

REINDEER GAMES

Question: "What do the female reindeer do when Santa takes the male reindeer out on Christmas Eve?"

Answer: "They go into town and blow a few bucks!"

CHECKMATE

Question: "What do you call a bunch of grandmasters of chess bragging about their games in a hotel lobby?"

Answer: "Chess nuts boasting in an open foyer!"

IT'S A CRACKER

Question: "What do elves use to go from floor to floor?"

Answer: "An Elfevator!"

***

Ray Mears was filming an episode for one of his "How to survive" series, where he was supposed to camp overnight, out in the open next to a crocodile infested river.

The film crew recorded Ray setting up camp for the night then left him on his own whilst they retreated to the safety and luxury of their camping trailer for a proper hot meal and a warm comfortable bed.

Meanwhile, Ray Mears was by the riverside when unbeknown to him, there was a huge crocodile creeping upon him.

Ray turned round, but it was too late, the croc swallowed Ray until all you could see was his head.

It was at this point that a member of the film crew, who having realized he had left a valuable piece of equipment near Ray's camp and had gone back to fetch it, saw the crocodile with just Ray's head sticking out.

Upon his return to the trailer, he said to the rest of the crew, "That Ray Mears is a cheat, I've just gone back to his camp and he is laying there in one of those designer Lacoste sleeping bags!"

An Englishman, who was down on his luck and had lost everything, decided to move on.

He bought himself a remote farm way out in the prairies of Texas.

He had been working his farm in total solitude for twelve months when one day there came a knock at his door.

He opened the door to be greeted by the sight of a shortish kind of guy sporting a pair of denim dungarees, a check shirt and a straw hat, who had a grin that stretched from ear to ear, exposing the odd gap where his teeth were missing.

"Howdy," he said, "I'm your neighbor and I'm having a party at the weekend and you are most welcome to come. There will be plenty of eating, drinking, dancing and wild rampant sex!"

"Oh great," said the Englishman, "I'd love to come on over, but I'm not sure what to wear!"

"That's up to you," said his neighbor, "there will only be the two of us."

***

A blonde walks into a Chemist and says to the assistant behind the counter, "Can I have some bottom deodorant please?"

"I'm sorry," replied the assistant, but we do not sell such a product.

"But you do," said the blonde rather indignantly, "I always buy it here!"

"Have you got an old one that you can bring in?" asked the assistant, "so I can identify it?"

The blonde leaves the Chemist's shop, only to return some hours later clutching an old stick deodorant. She goes back to the same counter and the same assistant and says, "here you are, this is the deodorant that I want."

"Oh," said the assistant, "this is just an ordinary stick deodorant."

"That's where you're wrong," said the blonde, "if you read the instructions, it says remove cap and push up bottom!"

***

A man walks into a pub, orders a pint and asks for it to be put on the slate whilst at the same time he places on the bar a large round tin and on the lid puts a duck which starts to dance.

Several pints later he thinks about leaving only to discover that he can not pay his bar bill, as he does not have a penny in cash or a plastic card with him.

He tells the landlord of his predicament and offers the tin and the dancing duck as a form of settlement.

The landlord thinks for a few minutes and then he accepts, thinking the dancing duck will bring in the crowds to the pub.

Later that night, the last person left in the pub, drinks up and leaves, the landlord locks all the doors, switches off the lights and goes upstairs to his flat over the pub and goes to bed.

However, he cannot get to sleep, because of the constant drumming of the ducks feet on the tin. Finally, out of sheer frustration, he phones the man who gave him the tin and the duck to explain the situation.

The man simply replies, "Oh didn't I tell you, all you need to do is remove the lid and blow out the candle!"

***

There was this baby brown paper bag, who one day was not feeling very well and decided to go to the doctor's.

When he arrives at the doctor's, the doctor says, "Hello, baby brown paper bag, what can I do for you?"

The paper bag says to the doctor, "I'm not feeling well."

The doctor carries out some tests and instructions and tells the paper bag to come back in a week's time when the results of the tests should be back.

So a week later the paper bag goes back to see the doctor.

The doctor said to the paper bag, "The results of the test show that you have avian or bird flu, have you been used to carry or wrap any poultry meat in?"

"Certainly not," said the paper bag, "I am brand new; I have not been used for anything!"

"In that case," the doctor replied, "your mother must have been a carrier!"

A husband and wife go on a week's holiday, staying in a log cabin by a lake.

Each day, the husband goes off in his little rowing boat to do some fishing, whilst his wife stayed behind drinking her favorite brand of coffee and reading her way through the pile of romantic novels she had taken with her.

One day, the husband decides to have a break from fishing, so his wife decides that she would give the peace and tranquility of the lake a try.

She prepares a flask of coffee, some sandwiches, grabs a couple of books, gets the boat, and rows to a point way off shore, drops anchor, pours herself a coffee, settles down and starts to read one of her books.

After a short while a small boat comes alongside and the ranger on board says, "Good morning, ma'am, what are you doing? You are in a restricted fishing zone!"

"I am not doing any harm," she said, "I'm just drinking coffee and reading a book."

The ranger who had spotted all of her husband's fishing gear still in the boat said, "Well what's to stop you fishing, you have got all of the equipment."

The woman replied, "In that case, I'll report you for sexual harassment!"

"But, I haven't done anything," said the ranger.

"You've got all the equipment," the woman said. "What's to stop you!"

***

Adam was wandering around the Garden of Eden one day, feeling bored and extremely lonely.

So he looks up to the Heavens and asks God if there is anything he can do.

God replies, "Of course there is. I will make a companion for you called Woman, she will prepare all your food, clean your house, do your washing, bear you children and satisfy your every need."

"Great," says Adam, "but what will this cost me?"

"An arm and a leg," replies God.

"What do I get for, let's say, 'a rib?'" inquires Adam.

The rest, as they say, is history

***

A FRENCHMAN, A SCOTSMAN AND AN IRISHMAN

Three dead bodies turn up at the mortuary, all with very big smiles on their faces.

The Coroner calls in the Police to tell them what has happened.

"First body: Frenchman, sixty, died of heart failure while making love to his mistress. Hence the enormous smile, Inspector," says the Coroner.

"Second body: Scotsman, twenty-five, won a thousand pounds on the lottery, spent it all on whisky, died of alcohol poisoning, hence the smile."

The Inspector asks, "What about the third body?"

"Ah," says the Coroner, "this is the most unusual one: big Seamus Quinn from Donegal, thirty, struck by lightening."

"Why is he smiling then?" inquires the Inspector.

"Thought he was having his photo taken," replies the Coroner.

***

An Irishman was terribly overweight, so his doctor put him on a diet.

"I want you to eat regularly for two days, then skip a day, and repeat this procedure for two weeks, and the next time I see you, you should have lost at least five pounds!"
When the Irishman returned two weeks later, he shocked the doctor by having lost nearly sixty pounds!

"Why, that's amazing! Did you follow my instructions?" asked the doctor.

The Irishman nodded. "I'll tell you, though, bejaysus, I tort I were going to drop dead on dat der tird day, drop dead!"

"From the hunger, you mean?" asked the doctor.

"No," said the Irishman, "from all the feckin skippin!"

***

A young man starts a new job at his local zoo and is given three tasks.

First he has to clear the weeds from the exotic fish pool. As he is doing this, a piranha jumps out and bites him. In a panic, he beats the fish to death with a spade. Realising his employer won't be best pleased with his actions, he disposes of the fish by feeding it to the lions, as lions will eat anything.

Moving on to the second job of cleaning out the primate house, he is attacked by two aggressive chimpanzees, who pelt him with coconuts. He swipes wildly at the chimps with his spade, killing them both. What can he do? Feed them to the lions, of course, because lions eat anything. He hurls the corpses into the lion enclosure.

He moved to his last job, which is to collect honey from South American Bees. As soon as he starts, he is attacked by a swarm of angry bees. He grabs the spade and smashes hundreds of them to a pulp. He throws the squashed dead bees into the lion enclosure, because the lions will eat anything.

Later that day, a new lion arrives at the zoo. He wanders up to the other lions and asks, "What's the food like here?"

One of the other lions reply, "Absolutely brilliant, today we had fish, chimps and mushy bees!"

***

After having their eleventh child, a couple from Liverpool decided that was enough, as the social wouldn't buy them a bigger bed and they weren't strong enough to steal one.

The husband went to see his doctor, and told him that he and his wife didn't want to have any more children.

The doctor told him there was a procedure called a vasectomy that would fix the problem, but it was expensive.

A less costly alternative was to go home, get a firework, light it, put it in a beer can, then hold the can up to his ear and count to ten.

The Scouser said to the doctor, "I may not be the smartest guy in the world, but I don't see how putting a firework in a beer can next to my ear is going to help me!"

"Trust me, it will do the job," said the doctor.

So that night the man went home, lit a banger and put it into a beer can. He held the can up to his ear and began to count: "1, 2, 3, 4, 5," at which point he paused, placed the beer can between his legs so he could continue counting on his other hand.

It is believed that this procedure is also known to work in Middlesborough, part of Bradford and the whole of Wales!

WHAT A COINCIDENCE!

A chicken farmer went to a local bar, sat next to a woman and ordered a glass of champagne.

The woman perks up and says, "How about that? I too have just ordered a glass of champagne!"

"What a coincidence," says the farmer. "This is a special day for me, I'm celebrating!"

"Today is a special day for me also and I too am celebrating," replies the woman.

"Well what a coincidence," says the farmer.

As they clinked glasses, the farmer asks, "What are you celebrating?"

"My husband and I have been trying for years to have a child, and today my gynaecologist told me that I'm pregnant!"

"What a coincidence," says the farmer, "I'm a chicken farmer and for years all of my hens have been infertile, but today they're finally laying eggs."

"That's great!" says the woman, "How did your chickens become fertile?"

"I used a different cock," replies the chicken farmer.

The woman just smiled and says, "What a coincidence!"

***

There was an aging woman, Mildred. She was ninety-three years old and was particularly despondent over the recent death of her husband, Earl, so she decided that she was going to kill herself and join him in death.

Thinking that it would be best to get it over with quickly, she took out Earl's old army pistol and made the decision to shoot herself in the heart, since it was so badly broken at the loss over her loved one!

Not wanting to miss the vital organ and become a vegetable and be a burden to someone, she called her doctor's office to enquire as to just exactly where the heart would be on a woman.

The doctor said, "Your heart would be just below your left breast!"

Later that night, Mildred was admitted to hospital with gunshot wounds to her left knee!

***

Five surgeons from big cities are discussing who makes the best patients to operate on.

The first surgeon, from Manchester, says, "I like to see accountants on my operating table, because when you open them up, everything inside is numbered!"

The second, from Birmingham, responds, "Yeah, but you should try electricians! Everything inside them is colour coded!"

The third surgeon, from Edinburgh, says, "No, I really think librarians are the best, as everything inside them is in alphabetical order!"

The fourth surgeon, from Belfast, chimes in, "You know, I like construction workers, these guys always understand when you have a few parts left over!"

The fifth surgeon, from London, shuts them all up, when he observes, "You're all wrong, politicians are by far the easiest to operate on. There's no guts, no heart, no balls, no brain, no spine, and the head and the arse are interchangeable!"

***

A man met a beautiful blonde lady and decided he wanted to marry her right away.

She said, "But we don't know anything about each other."

He said "That's okay, we'll learn about each other as we go along."

So, she consented, they were married, and off they went on honeymoon at a very nice resort.

One morning, while they were laying by the pool, the man got up off of his towel, climbed up to the ten meter board and did a two and a half tuck, followed by three rotations in the pike position, at which point he straightened out and cut the water like a knife.

After a few more demonstrations, he came back and lay down on his towel.
She said, "That was incredible!"

The man replied, "I used to be an Olympic diving champion. You see, I told you we'd learn more about each other as we went along!"

A little while later, she got up, jumped in the pool, and started doing lengths. After seventy-five, she climbed out of the pool, lay back down on her towel and was hardly out of breath.

The man said, "That was incredible! Were you an Olympic endurance swimmer?"

"No," she said, "I was a prostitute in Liverpool, but I worked both sides of the river Mersey!"

***

WOMEN'S LOVE POEM

Before I lay me down to sleep,

I pray for a man, who is not a creep,

One who's handsome, smart and strong

One who loves to listen long,

One who thinks before he speaks,

One who'll call, not wait for weeks.

I pray he's gainfully employed,

When I spend his cash, won't be annoyed.

Pulls out my chair and opens my door,

Massages my back and begs to do more.

Oh! Send me a man who'll make love to my mind,

Knows what to answer to "How big is my behind?"

I pray that this man will love me to no end,

And always be my very best friend.

MARTIN ELBROW

MEN'S LOVE POEM

I pray for a deaf-mute nymphomaniac with

Huge boobs who owns a bar on a golf course,

And loves to send me fishing and hunting. This

doesn't rhyme and I don't give a s**t.

69

ARE YOU DEAF OR WHAT?

A man feared his wife Peg wasn't hearing as well as she used to and he thought she might need a hearing aid. Not quite sure how to approach her on the subject, he called the family doctor to discuss the problem.

The doctor told him there is a simple, yet informal test the husband could perform to give the doctor a better idea about her hearing loss.

"Here's what you do," said the doctor. "Stand about forty feet away from her, and in a normal conversational speaking tone see if she hears you, if not go to thirty feet, then twenty feet, and so on until you get a response."

That evening, Peg was in the kitchen, cooking dinner, and he was in the den. He says to himself, "I'm about forty feet away, let's see what happens." Then in a normal tone he asks, "Honey, what's for dinner?"

No response.

So he moves closer to the kitchen, about thirty feet from his wife and repeats, "Peg, what's for dinner?"

Still there was no response.

Next he moves into the dining room where he is about twenty feet away from his wife and asks, "Honey, what's for dinner?"

Again he gets no response.

So, he walks up to the kitchen door, by now he is only about ten feet away. "Honey, what's for dinner?"

Again there is no response.

So he walks right up behind her and says, "Peg, what's for dinner?"

(You'll just love this)

"Frank, for the FIFTH time, it's CHICKEN!"

BEER CONTAINS FEMALE HORMONES

Last month, The National University of Lesotho scientists released the results of a recent analysis that revealed the presence of female hormones in beer.

Men should take a concerned look at their beer consumption.

The theory is that beer contains female hormones (hops contain phytoestrogens) and that by drinking enough beer, men turn into women.

To test the theory, one hundred men each drank eight pints of beer within a one hour period.

It was then observed that one hundred percent of the test subjects:

Argued over nothing;

Refused to apologise when obviously wrong;

Gained weight;

Talked excessively without making sense;

Became overly emotional;

Couldn't drive;

Failed to think rationally;

Had to sit down while urinating.

No further testing was considered necessary.

Let this be a warning to all men who drink too much beer!

WOMEN'S ARSE SIZE STUDY

There is a new study just released by the Psychiatric Association about women and how they feel about their arses.

The results are pretty interesting:

Five percent of all women surveyed feel their arse is too big.

Ten percent of all women surveyed feel their arse is too small.

The remaining eighty five percent say they don't care; they love him; he's a good man, and they would have married him anyway!

An Irishman walks into a bar in Dublin, orders three pints of Guinness, and sits in the back of the room, drinking a sip out of each glass in turn. When he finished all three, he comes back to the bar and orders three more. The bartender says to him, "You know, a pint goes flat after I draw it, it would taste better if you bought one at a time."

The Irishman replies, "Well, you see, I have two brothers, one in America, the other in Australia, and I'm here in Dublin. When we all left home, we promised that we would drink this way to remember the days we all drank together."

The bartender admits that this is a nice custom, and leaves it there.

The Irishman becomes a regular in the bar and always drinks the same way: He orders three pints and drinks the three pints by taking a drink from each one in turn.

One day, he comes in and orders two pints. All the other regulars in the bar notice and fall silent.

When he comes back to the bar for the second round, the bartender says, "I don't want to intrude on your grief, but I wanted to offer my condolences on your great loss."

The Irishman looks confused for a moment, then the light dawns in his eye and he laughs.

"Oh, no," he says. "Everyone is fine. It's me...I've quit drinking!"

***

A woman went into a pet shop and immediately spotted a large, beautiful parrot.

There was a sign on the cage that read fifty pounds.

"Why such a low price?" she asked the pet shop owner.

The owner looked at her and said, "Look, I should tell you first that this bird used to live in a house of Prostitution and sometimes it says some pretty vulgar stuff."

The woman thought about this, but decided she had to have the bird anyway. She took it home and hung the bird's cage in her living room and waited for it to say something.

The bird looked around the room, then at her, and said, "New house, new madam."

The woman was a bit shocked at the implication, but then thought that it really wasn't that bad.

When her two teenage daughters returned from school, the bird saw them and said, "New house, new madam, new girls."

The girls and the woman were a bit offended, but then began to laugh about the situation, considering how and where the parrot had been raised.

Moments later, the woman's husband Keith came home from work.

The bird looked at him and said, "Hi Keith!"

***

An Italian, a Scotsman and a Chinese man, are all hired to work on a construction site.

The foreman points to a huge pile of sand.

He says to the Italian guy, "You're in charge of sweeping."

To the Scotsman he says, "You're in charge of shoveling."

And to the Chinese guy, "You're in charge of supplies."

He then says, "Now I have to leave for a little while, I expect you men to make a dent in that pile of sand."

So when the foreman returns after being away for a couple of hours, the pile of sand is untouched.

He asks the Italian, "Why didn't you sweep any of it?"

The Italian relies, "I no hava no broom, you saida to the Chinese fella that he wasa ina charge of supplies, but he hasa disappeared and I no coulda find him nowhere."

Then the foreman turns to the Scotsman and says "And you, I thought I told you to shovel this pile."

The Scotsman replies, "Aye, that ye did laddie, boot ah couldna fin' him neither."

The foreman is really angry now.

He storms off towards the pile of sand to look for the Chinese gent.

Just then, the Chinese man leaps out from behind the pile of sand and yells, "SUPPLIES!!!!!!"

A husband and wife are shopping in their local supermarket, when the husband picks up a crate of Stella and puts it in their trolley.

"What do you think you are doing?" asks the wife.

"They're on offer, only ten pounds for twelve cans," he replies.

"Put them back, we can't afford them," demands the wife, and so they carry on with the shopping.

A few aisles further along, the woman picks up a jar of face cream priced at twenty pounds and sticks it in the trolley.

"What do you think you are doing?" asks the husband.

"It's my face cream.... It makes me look beautiful," replies the wife. To which her husband retorts, "SO DOES TWELVE CANS OF STELLA — AND ITS HALF THE PRICE!"

***

GOLFER AT THE DENTIST

A man and his wife walked into reception at their dental surgery. The man said to the dentist, "Doc, I'm in one hell of a hurry. I have two buddies sitting out in my car waiting for us to go play golf, so forget about the anesthetic and just pull the tooth and be done with it. We have a 10:00 a.m. tee time at the best golf course in town and it is 9:30 already. I don't have time to wait for the anesthetic to work.

The dentist thought to himself, *My goodness, this is surely a very brave man asking to have his tooth pulled, without using anything to kill the pain.* So the dentist asked him, "Which tooth is it, sir?"

The man turned to his wife and said, "Open your mouth, honey, and show him."

IT JUST GOES TO SHOW THAT YOU ARE NEVER TOO OLD

A couple, who are well into their eighties, go to a sex therapist's office.

The therapist asks, "What can I do for you?"

The man says, "Will you watch us have sexual intercourse?"

The therapist raises both eyebrows, but he is so amazed that such an elderly couple are asking for sexual advice that he agrees.

When the couple finish, the therapist says, "There is absolutely nothing wrong with the way you have intercourse." He thanks them for coming to see him, wishes them good luck, charges them fifty pounds, and bids them good day.

The next week, however, the couple returns and asks the sex therapist to watch again. He is a bit puzzled, but agrees.

This happens several weeks in a row, the couple make an appointment, have intercourse with no problems, pay the therapist and then leave.

Finally, after several weeks of this routine, the therapist says, "I'm sorry , but I have to ask, just what are you trying to find out?"

The old man says, "We're not trying to find out anything. She's married and we can't go to her house. I'm married and we can't go to my house. Travelodge charge ninety three pounds. The Hilton charges one hundred and thirty nine pounds. We do it here for fifty pounds, and I get forty three pounds back from Bupa.

BEAR IN A BAR

A bear walks into a bar in Billings, Montana. He bangs on the bar with his paw and demands a beer.

The bartender approaches and says, "We don't serve beer to bears in bars in Billings."

The bear, becoming angry, demands again that he be served a beer.

The bartender tells him again, more forcefully, "We don't serve beer to belligerent bears in bars in Billings."

The bear, very angry now, says, "If you don't serve me a beer, I'm going to eat that lady sitting at the end of the bar."

The bartender says, "Sorry, we don't serve beer to belligerent, bully bears in bars in Billings."

The bear goes to the end of the bar and, as promised, eats the woman. He comes back to his seat and again demands a beer.

The bartender states, "Sorry, we don't serve beer to belligerent, bully bears in bars in Billings who are on drugs."

The bear says "I'm not on drugs."

... Wait for it!...

The bartender says, "You are now. That was a barbitchyouate."

CALL CENTRES

You either love them or loathe them, some excerpts from actual call centre conversations have been included for your amusement. Names have been omitted to protect the offenders taking part in these calls.

Customer: "I've been ringing 0800 2100 for two days and can't get through to enquiries, can you help?"

Operator: "Where did you get that number from, sir?"

Customer: "It was on the door to the Travel Centre."

Operator: "Sir, they are our opening hours."

A CALL TO A MANUFACTURER OF A WELL KNOWN BRAND OF ELECTRONIC CONSUMER GOODS

Caller: "Can you give me the telephone number for Jack?"

Operator: "I'm sorry, sir, I don't understand who you are talking about."

Caller: "On page one, section five, of the user guide it clearly states that I need to unplug the fax machine from the AC wall socket and telephone Jack before cleaning. Now, can you give me the number for Jack?"

Operator: "I think you will find it means the telephone point on the wall."

A CALL TO A WELL KNOWN MOTORING ORGANIZATION

Caller: "Does your European Breakdown Policy cover me when I am travelling in Australia?"

Operator: "Doesn't the product name give you a clue?"

***

Caller: (Enquiring about legal requirements while travelling in France): "If I register my car in France, do I have to change the steering wheel to the other side of the car?"

DIRECTORY ENQUIRIES

Caller: "I'd like the number of the Argoed Fish Bar in Cardiff please."

Operator: "I'm sorry, there's no listing. Is the spelling correct?"

Caller: "Well, it used to be called the Bargoed Fish Bar, but the 'B' fell off."

***

Then there was a caller who asked for a knitwear company in woven.

Operator: "Woven? Are you sure?"

Caller: "Yes. That's what it says on the label; Woven in Scotland."

FOR ALL YOU TECHIES WITH A SENSE OF HUMOUR!

FIRST CALL

Tech Support: "I need you to right-click on the Open Desktop."

Customer: "Okay."

Tech Support: "Did you get a pop-up menu?"

Customer: "No."

Tech Support: "Okay. Right-click again. Do you see a pop-up menu?"

Customer: "No."

Tech Support: "Okay, sir, can you tell me what you have done up until this point?"

Customer: "Sure, you told me to write 'click' and I wrote 'click.'"

SECOND CALL

Tech Support: "Okay. In the bottom lefthand side of the screen, can you see the 'OK' button displayed?"

Customer: "Wow. How can you see my screen from there?"

THIRD CALL

Caller: "I deleted a file from my PC last week and I have just realized that I need it. If I turn my system clock back two weeks will I have my file back again?"

LITTLE JOHNNY STRIKES AGAIN

The teacher asked the class to use the word 'fascinate' in a sentence.

Molly put her hand up and said, "My family went to my Granddad's farm and we all saw his pet sheep. It was fascinating."

The teacher said, "Very good, Molly, but I wanted you to use the word fascinate, not fascinating!"

Sally raised her hand and said, "My family went to see The Eden Project and I was fascinated."

The teacher said, "Well that was also good Sally, but I wanted you to use the word fascinate."
Little Johnny raised his hand, and the teacher hesitated for a moment as she had been burned by Little Johnny before. She finally decided there was no way he could damage the word fascinate, so she asked him to read out his sentence.

Johnny said, "My Aunt Gina has a sweater with ten buttons, but her tits are so big she can only fasten eight."

The teacher just sat down and cried!

***

LOVE & MARRIAGE

There was this guy called Rick, and he had forgotten his wedding anniversary.

Needless to say, his wife was really very angry, and she told him, "Tomorrow morning, I expect to find a gift in the driveway that goes from zero to two hundred in less than six seconds... AND IT HAD BETTER BE THERE!'

The next morning, Rick got up early and left for work.

When his wife woke up, she looked out of the bedroom window, and sure enough, there was a gift-wrapped box in the middle of the drive.

Confused, the wife put on her dressing gown, ran out to the driveway and brought the box back into the house, where she ripped off the gift-wrap in eager anticipation, opened the box, only to find a brand new pair of bathroom scales.

Rick has been missing since last Friday!

***

CONTINUING ON THE MARRIAGE THEME

An elderly married couple go into a burger bar, and the husband places an order for one hamburger with French fries and a drink.

Having been given the meal for one, the couple went and sat at a table, where the husband unwrapped the hamburger and carefully cut it in half, placing one half in front of his wife.

He then proceeded to count out the French fries, placing them into two piles, one in front of his wife, and the other in front of himself.

He placed the drink between them, and they took it in turns to take sips from it.

As he began to eat his half of the burger, the people sat around them were looking over and whispering.

Obviously they were thinking that the old couple were poor, and could only afford to buy one meal between the two of them.

As the man began to eat his fries, a young man came to the table and politely offered to buy another meal for them.

The husband thanked him and said they were just fine, and that they were used to sharing everything.

People closer to the table also noticed that the wife had not eaten any of her share of the meal. She just sat there watching her husband eat and occasionally take her turn in sipping at the drink.

Once again, the young man came over and begged them to let him buy another meal for them.

This time, the wife said, "No, thank you, we are used to sharing everything!"

Finally, as the husband finished and was wiping his face with a napkin, the young man again came over to the wife, who had yet to eat a bite of her meal and asked, "What is it you are waiting for?"

The wife simply replied, "It's my turn with the teeth!"

STILL ON THE SUBJECT OF MARRIAGE:
THE ELEVENTH HUSBAND?

A young man married a beautiful woman, who had previously divorced ten husbands.

On their wedding night, she said to her new husband, "Please be gentle with me as I'm still a virgin!"

"What?" asked the puzzled groom. "How can that be, if you have been married ten times?"

With that, she began to tell all about her experiences with the ten previous husbands, and this is how it went!

"Well, husband No. 1 was a sales representative, he just kept telling me how great it was going to be.

"As for husband No. 2, he was in software services, he was never really sure how it was supposed to function, told me that he would look into it and get back to me.

"Then there was husband No. 3, he was from field services, he claimed that everything checked out diagnostically, but he just could not get the system up.

"Husband No. 4 was in telemarketing, even though he knew he had the order, he didn't know when he would be able to deliver.

"Of course, husband No. 5 was an engineer, he understood the basic process but wanted three years to research, implement, and design a new state-of-the-art method."

"With husband No. 6, he was in administration, he thought he knew how, but was never sure whether it was his job or not.

"Now husband No. 7 was in marketing, although he had a product, he was never sure how to position it.

"Husband No. 8 was a psychiatrist, all he ever did was talk about it.

"Husband No. 9 was a gynaecologist, all he ever wanted to do was look at it.

"My husband No. 10 was a stamp collector, all he ever did was… Oh God, how I miss him! But now, my darling, I have married you, husband No. 11, and I'm so excited!"

"That's wonderful," said the husband, "but can I ask why?"

"Because you are with the government, this time I know I'm going to get screwed!"

***

This next lucky chap had a narrow escape!

THE GOOD HUSBAND

Jack wakes up with a huge hangover, after attending his company's Christmas bash. Now Jack is not normally a drinker, but the drinks didn't taste like alcohol at all.

He did not even remember how he got home from the party, and as bad as he was feeling, he wondered if he did something wrong.

Jack had to force himself to open his eyes, and the first thing he sees is a couple of aspirins next to a glass of water on the side table, there was also a single red rose. Jack sits up and sees his clothing in front of him, all clean and pressed.

He looks around the room and sees that it is in perfect order, spotlessly clean, so is the rest of the house.

He takes the aspirins, cringes when he sees a huge black eye staring back at him in the bathroom mirror.

Then he notices a note hanging on the corner of the mirror written in red with little hearts on it and a kiss mark from his wife in lipstick.

The note reads: "Honey, breakfast is on the stove, I left early to get groceries to make you your favourite dinner tonight. I love you darling! Love Jillian. XX"

He stumbles down to the kitchen, where sure enough, there is hot breakfast, a pot of steaming hot coffee, and the morning newspaper.

His son is also at the table, eating his breakfast.

Jack asks, "Son, what happened last night?"

"Well you came home around 3 a.m., drunk and totally out of your mind. You fell over the coffee table and broke it, and then you threw up in the hallway, and got a black eye when you ran into the door."

Confused, he asked his son, "So, why is everything in such perfect order and so clean? I have a rose, and breakfast is on the table waiting for me?"

His son replies, "Oh that!... Mum dragged you to the bedroom, and when she tried to take your pants off, you screamed, LEAVE ME ALONE, I'M MARRIED!"

***

NOW THAT'S WHAT I CALL AN IRISH COFFEE!

An Irish woman of some advancing years, visited her GP to seek his help in reviving her husband's libido.

"What about trying Viagra?" asked the doctor.

"Not a chance," she replied, "he won't even take an aspirin."

"Not a problem," said the doctor. "Give him an Irish soluble Viagra. Drop it into his coffee. He won't even taste it. Give it a try and call me in a week to let me know how things went."

Well, it wasn't even a week, when she called the doctor, who directly inquired as to what progress had been made.

The poor dear exclaimed, "Oh, faith, bejaysus, begorrah! 'T was horrid, Just terrible doctor!"

"Really? What exactly happened?" asked the doctor.

"Well I did as you advised and slipped it in his coffee and the effect was almost immediate. He jumped his self straight up, with a twinkle in his eye, and with his pants bulgin fiercely!"

With one swoop of his arm, he sent the cups and tablecloth flyin, ripped me clothes to tatters and took me then and there, making wild, mad passionate love to me on the tabletop! It was a nightmare, I tell you an absolute feckin nightmare!"

"Why so terrible?" asked the doctor. "Do you mean the sex that your husband provided wasn't good?"

"Oh, no, no no, doctor, the sex was fine indeed! 'T was the best sex I've had in fifty years of marriage! But sure as I'm sittin' here, I'll niver be able to show me face in Starbucks again!"

BOB'S LITTLE PROBLEM

The doctor said to his patient Bob, "Of course I won't laugh, I'm a professional. In over twenty years as a GP, I've never laughed at a patient."

"Okay then," Bob said and proceeded to drop his trousers, revealing the tiniest piece of wedding tackle the doc had ever seen. It could not have been any bigger than the size of an AAA battery.

Unable to control himself, the doctor started giggling, then fell to the floor, in uncontrollable fits of laughter. Ten minutes later, he struggled to his feet and regained his composure.

"I'm so sorry," said the doctor. "I just don't know quite what came over me. On my honour as both a doctor and a gentleman, I promise it won't happen again. Now, what seems to be the problem?"

"It's swollen!" Bob replied.

FIVE TIPS FOR A WOMAN

It is important that a man helps you around the house and has a job.

It is important that a man makes you laugh.

It is important to find a man you can count on and doesn't lie to you.

It is important that a man loves you and spoils you.

It is important that these four men don't know each other.

***

FOOT NOTE

One saggy boob said to the other saggy boob:

"If we don't get some support soon, people will think we're nuts!"

***

ONE FOR THE GIRLS

Now I lay me down to sleep

I pray the Lord my shape to keep.

Please no wrinkles, please no bags

And please lift my butt before it sags.

Please no age spots, please no grey,

And as for my belly, please take it away.

Please keep me healthy, please keep me young,

And thank you dear lord, for all that you've done.

***

Did I Read That Sign Correctly?

RECENTLY IN THE GENTS TOILETS IN A WELL KNOWN LOCAL DEPARTMENT STORE

Toilet out of order. Please use the floor below.

IN A LONDON DEPARTMENT STORE

Bargain Basement Upstairs.

IN A LAUNDROMAT

Automatic washing machines: Please remove all your clothes when the light goes out.

IN AN OFFICE

Would the person who took the step ladder yesterday please bring it back or further steps will be taken.

After tea break staff should empty the teapot and stand upside down on the draining board.

OUTSIDE A SECONDHAND SHOP

We exchange anything—bicycles, washing machines, etc. Why not bring your wife along and get a wonderful bargain.

NOTICE IN A HEALTH FOOD SHOP

Closed due to Illness.

NOTICE IN A FARMERS FIELD

The Farmer allows walkers to cross the field for free, but the bull charges.

MESSAGE ON A LEAFLET

If you cannot read, this leaflet will tell you how to get lessons.

ON A REPAIR SHOP DOOR

We can repair anything. (Please knock hard on the door – the bell doesn't work).

SPOTTED IN A SAFARI PARK (I SURE HOPE SO)

Elephants, please stay in your car.

ANOTHER CALL CENTRE CORKER

One of the best so far. There's always one. This has got to be one of the funniest things in a long time. This guy should have been promoted, not fired. This is a true story from the Word Perfect helpline, which has been transcribed from a recording monitoring the customer care department. Needless to say the help desk employee was fired (Now I know why they record these calls!):

Operator: "Good afternoon, how may I help you?"

Caller: "Yes, well, I'm having trouble with WordPerfect."

Operator: "What sort of trouble?"

Caller: "Well, I was just typing along, and all of a sudden, the words went away."

Operator: "Went away?"

Caller: "They disappeared."

Operator: "Hmm, so what does your screen look like now?"

Caller: "Nothing."

Operator: "Nothing?"

Caller: "It's blank, it won't accept anything when I type."

Operator: "Are you still in WordPerfect, or did you get out?"

Caller: "How do I tell?"

Operator: "Can you see the C prompt on the screen?"

Caller: "What's the sea prompt?"

Operator: "Never mind, can you move your cursor around the screen?"

Caller: "There isn't any cursor, I told you, it won't accept anything I type."

Operator: "Does your monitor have a power indicator?"

Caller: "What's a monitor?"

Operator: "It's the thing with the screen on it that looks like a TV. Does it have a little light that tells you when its on?"

Caller: "I don't know."

Operator: "Well then, look on the back of the monitor and find where the power cord goes into it. Can you see that?"

Caller: "Yes, I think so."

Operator: "Great, follow the lead to the plug, and tell me if its plugged into the wall."

Caller: "Yes it is."

Operator: "When you were behind the monitor, did you notice if there were two cables plugged into the back of it, not just one?"

Caller: "No."

Operator: "Well there are. I need you to look back there again and find the other cable."

Caller: "Okay, here it is."

Operator: "Follow it for me and tell me if it is plugged securely into the back of your computer."

Caller: "I can't reach."

Operator: "Uh huh. Well can you see if it is?"

Caller: "No."

Operator: "Even if you put your knee on something and lean way over?"

Caller: "Oh it's not because I don't have the right angle, its because it is dark."

Operator: "Dark?"

Caller: "Yes, the office light is off, and the only light I have is coming in the window."

Operator: "Well turn on the office light then."

Caller: "I can't."

Operator: "No? Why not?"

Caller: "Because there's a power failure."

Operator: "A power...a power failure? Aha, Ok, we've got it licked now. Do you still have the boxes and manuals and packing stuff your computer came in?"

Caller: "Well, yes, I keep them in the closet."

Operator: "Good. Go get them, and unplug your system and pack it up just like it was when you got it. Then take it back to the store you bought it from."
Caller: "Really? Is it that bad?"

Operator: "Yes, I'm afraid it is."

Caller: "Well all right then, I suppose. What do I tell them."

Operator: "Tell them you're too f*****g stupid to own a computer!"

***

BAD PARROT

There was this young man called John, and he received a parrot as a gift. Now this parrot had a bad attitude and an even worse vocabulary. Every word that came out of the bird's beak was rude, obnoxious, and laced with profanity.

John tried and tried to change the bird's attitude by consistently saying only polite words, playing soft music and anything else he could think of to do, that would 'clean up' the birds vocabulary.

Finally John was fed up and he yelled at the parrot. The parrot yelled back.

John shook the parrot and the parrot got angrier and even ruder. John, in desperation, threw up his hand, grabbed the bird and put him in the freezer.

For a few minutes the parrot squawked and kicked and screamed. Then suddenly there was total quiet. Not a peep was heard for over a minute. Fearing that he'd hurt the parrot, John quickly opened the door to the freezer. The parrot calmly stepped out onto John's outstretched arm and said, "I believe I may have offended you with my rude language and actions. I'm sincerely remorseful for my inappropriate transgressions and I fully intend to do everything I can to correct my rude and unforgivable behavior."

John was stunned at the change in the bird's attitude. As he was about to ask the parrot what had made such a dramatic change in his behavior, the bird continued, "May I ask what the turkey did?"

***

A man was riding his Harley Davidson bike along a California beach when, suddenly, the sky clouded over above his head and, in a booming voice, the Lord said, "Because you have tried to be faithful to me in all ways, I will grant you one wish."

The biker pulled over and said, "Build a bridge to Hawaii, so I can ride over anytime I want."

The Lord said. "Your request is too materialistic, think of the enormous challenges for that kind of undertaking, the supports required to reach the bottom of the Pacific and the concrete and steel it would take! It will nearly exhaust several natural resources. I can do it, but it is hard for me to justify your desire for worldly things. Take a little more time and think of something that could possibly help mankind."

The biker thought about it for a long time. Finally, he said, "Lord, I wish that I and all men could understand our wives. I want to know how she feels inside, what she's thinking when she gives me the silent treatment, why she cries, what she means when she says nothing's wrong, and how can I make a woman truly happy?"

The Lord replied, "Was that two lanes or four that you wanted on that bridge?"

***

STAYING WITH THE BIKER/RELIGION/FEMALE THEME

The inventor of the Harley Davidson motorcycle, Arthur Davidson, died and went to heaven. At the Pearly Gates, St Peter told Arthur, "Since you've been such a good man and your motorcycles have changed the world, your reward is you can hang out with anyone you want to in heaven."

Arthur thought about this for a minute then said, "I want to hang out with God."

St Peter took Arthur to the throne room and introduced him to God.

God recognized Arthur and commented, "So you are the man who invented the Harley Davidson motorcycle?"

Arthur said, "Yeah, that's me."

God commented, "Well, what's the big deal inventing something that's pretty unstable, makes noise and pollution, and can't run without a road?"

Arthur was apparently embarrassed, but finally spoke, "Excuse me, but aren't you the inventor of woman?"

God said, "Ah yes."

"Well," said Arthur, "professional to professional, you have some major design flaws in your invention:

There's too much inconsistency in the front-end protrusion.

It chatters constantly at high speeds.

Most rear ends are too soft and wobble too much.

The intake is placed far too close to the exhaust.

The maintenance costs are outrageous."

"Hmmmmmmmmm, you may have some good points there," replied God, "But hold on."

God went to his celestial supercomputer, typed in a few words, and waited for the results. The computer printed out a slip of paper and God read it.

"Well, it may be true that my invention is flawed," God said to Arthur, "But according to these numbers, more men are riding my invention than yours!"

***

ONLY IN BRITAIN

Being British is about driving in a German car to an Irish pub for a Belgian beer, and then on the way home, grabbing an Indian curry or a Turkish kebab to eat, while sitting on Swedish furniture, watching American shows on a Japanese TV.

And the most British thing of all, suspicion of anything foreign!

Oh and… only in Britain, can a pizza get to your house faster than an ambulance!

Only in Britain… do supermarkets make sick people walk all the way to the back of the store to get their prescriptions, while 'healthy' people can buy cigarettes at the front!

Only in Britain… do people order double cheeseburgers, large fries and a **DIET** coke!

Only in Britain… do banks leave the doors wide open, yet chain the pens to the counter!

Only in Britain… do we leave cars worth thousands of pounds on the drive and lock our junk and cheap lawnmower in the garage!

Only in Britain… do we use answering machines to screen calls and then have call waiting so we won't miss a call from someone we didn't want to talk to in the first place!

Only in Britain… are there disabled parking places in front of a skating rink!

We might be British, but at least we have a sense of humour!

The Dog & Cat Diaries!

DOG DIARY

8:00 a.m. — Dog food! My favourite thing!

9:30 a.m. — A car ride! My favourite thing!

9:40 a.m. — A walk in the park! My favourite thing!

10:30 a.m. — Got rubbed and petted! My favourite thing!

12:00 p.m. — Lunch! My favourite thing!

1:00 p.m. — Played in the yard! My favourite thing!

5:00 p.m. — Milk bones! My favourite thing!

7:00 p.m. — Got to play ball! My favourite thing!

8:00 p.m. — Wow! Watched TV with the people! My favourite thing!

11:00 p.m. — Sleeping on the bed! My Favourite thing!

CAT DIARY

Day 983 of my captivity!

My captors continue to taunt me with bizarre little dangling objects!

They dine lavishly on fresh meat, while the other inmates and I are fed hash or some sort of dry nuggets. Although I make my contempt for the rations perfectly clear, I nevertheless must eat something in order to maintain my strength!

The only thing that keeps me going is my dream of escape. In an attempt to disgust them, I once again vomited on the carpet yesterday!

Today, I decapitated a mouse and dropped its headless body at their feet. I had hoped that this would strike fear into their hearts, since it clearly demonstrates what I am capable of. However, they merely made condescending comments about what a "good little hunter" I am!

There was some sort of family gathering and assembly of accomplices last night. I was placed in solitary confinement for the duration of the event. However, I could hear the noises and smell the food. I overheard that my confinement was due to some of their guests having 'cat allergies.' I must learn what this means, and how to use it to my advantage!

Today, I was almost successful in an attempt to assassinate one of my captor tormentors by weaving around his feet and between his legs as he was walking, but he somehow managed to avoid tripping over me. I must try again tomorrow, but at the top of the stairs!

I am convinced that the other prisoners here are flunkies and snitches, as the dog receives special privileges. He is regularly released and seems to be more than willing to return. He is obviously retarded.

The bird has got to be an informant, as I observe him communicating with the guards on a regular basis. I am certain the bird reports my every move as my captors have arranged protective custody for him in an elevated cell, so he is safe. For now!

***

OUT OF PETROL

A man was driving down the road and ran out of petrol.

Just at that moment, a bee flew in his window.

The bee asked, "What seems to be the problem?"

"I'm out of petrol!" the man replied.

The bee told the man to wait right there, and then flew off.

Minutes later, the man watched as an entire swarm of bees flew to his car and into his petrol tank. After a few minutes, the bees flew out again.

"Try it now," said the bee.

So the man turned the ignition key, and the engine started up.

"Wow!" exclaimed the man. "What did you put in my petrol tank?"

. . . Wait for it,

The bee answered, "BP."

***

"Waiter, Waiter, what's this fly doing in my soup?"

"It looks like breast stroke to me sir!"

NOT ANOTHER PARROT JOKE?

One day a man walked into a pet store to buy a parrot.

He found one that he liked and went up to the counter to buy it.

The sales assistant saw which parrot he had chosen and said, "That parrot repeats everything he hears."

"That's okay," the man replied as he paid for the bird and left the store.

As he was walking down the street, he saw a policeman chasing a robber.

The policeman shouted to his partner, "Shoot him down, Shoot him down!"

The parrot copied, shouting out loud, "Shoot him down, Shoot him down."

They carried on walking, and came across a man who was trying to jack his car up off the ground, because the wheels had been stolen.

The man said, "Pop it up, pop it up."

The parrot squawked, "Pop it up, pop it up."

They continued walking, and came to a fun fair. One of the stallholders at the funfair was yelling out to the crowd, "Hit a big one, and win a prize!"

The parrot said, "Hit a big one, and win a prize!"

The man and the parrot went into a church and sat down.

The priest was in the middle of his sermon.

He said, "The Lord is above us."

The parrot said, "Shoot him down, shoot him down!"

The priest continued, "The devil is below us!"

To which the parrot replied, "Pop it up, pop it up!"

By this time the priest started to get a little annoyed, and threw a bible at the parrot. The parrot ducked and the bible hit a fat lady behind him.

The parrot said in a loud voice, "Hit a big one, and win a prize!"

***

BUBBLE BLOWING DUCKIES

Three ducks were swimming in a pond after midnight and were arrested for trespassing. The next morning, they were called to appear in court.

The judge called in the first duck and asked, "What were you doing in the pond after midnight?"

"I was blowing bubbles," the first duck replied.

The judge called in the second duck and asked, "What were you doing in the pond after midnight?"

"I was blowing bubbles, Your Honour," replied the second duck.

The judge finally called in the third duck and said, "So let me guess, you were also blowing bubbles!"

"No," said the third duck, "I am Bubbles!"

***

One day, Jack says to Mike, "My elbow hurts like hell, I suppose I'd better go and see my doctor!"

"Listen mate, don't waste your time going to the surgery," Mike replies. "There's a diagnostic computer at the local supermarket. Just give it a urine sample, and the computer will tell you what's wrong and what to do about it. It takes about ten seconds and only costs a fiver… a lot quicker and better than a doctor and you will also get your Club Card points."

So Jack collects a urine sample in a jar and goes off to the local supermarket. He goes over to a booth, enters, and sits down, puts his five one pound coins in the slot, and the computer lights up and asks for the urine sample.

Jack pours the sample into the funnel, watches the liquid disappear, and sits back and waits. Ten seconds later, the computer produces a printout.

Its diagnosis reads, "You have tennis elbow. Soak your arm in warm water and avoid heavy activity. It will improve after approximately two weeks."

That evening, whilst thinking how amazing this new technology was, Jack begins to wonder if the computer could be fooled.

He mixed some tap water, a stool sample from his dog, urine samples from his wife and daughter, and pleasured himself into the mixture just for good measure.

Jack then hurries back to the local supermarket, goes to the booth and entered, pays his five pounds, and, eager to see what would happen, he pours in his concoction, and once again, sits back and awaits the results, whilst sporting a huge grin.

True to form, ten seconds later, the computer produces a printout, and the diagnosis read:

Your tap water is too hard. Get a water softener.

Your dog has ringworm. Bathe him with anti-fungal shampoo.

Your daughter has a cocaine habit. Get her into rehab.

Your wife is pregnant. Twins. They are not yours. Get a lawyer.

If you don't stop playing with yourself, your elbow will never get better.

Thank you for shopping with us today.

***

In a recent survey, people from Liverpool, have proven to be the most likely to have had sex in the shower!

In the survey, carried out for the manufacturers of top selling men's aftershave 'Brut,' a whopping eighty-six percent of Liverpudlians said they had enjoyed sex in the shower.

The other fourteen percent when asked, said they had never been to prison!

Eh. Eh. Eh. Calm down. Calm down.

***

SUCH BRAVADO!

A man charges into a bank wearing a balaclava and wielding a handgun.

He shouts, "This is a raid, everyone get down on the floor, do as you're told, and no one will get hurt!" He then proceeds to empty all of the cash drawers into a large bag.

As he runs towards the door with the loot, a brave customer yanks off the robber's balaclava. The robber immediately shoots the customer dead, and shouts, "Did anybody else here see my face?"

At which point the robber notices another customer peering from behind the counter, so he goes over and shoots him, too!

"Did anybody else see my face?" he shouts again, waving the gun around.

There is absolute silence, you could hear a pin drop, then, after a few moments, a male voice is heard from a distant corner...

"I think my missus caught a glimpse!"

***

An elderly couple who were both widowed had been going out with each other for a long time. Urged on by their friends and family, they decided it was finally time to get married. Before the wedding, they went out to dinner and had a long conversation, regarding how their marriage might work. They discussed finances, living arrangements, and so on. Finally, the old gentleman decided it was time to broach the subject of their physical relationship.

"How do you feel about sex?" he asked rather tentatively.

"I would like it infrequently," she replied.

The old gentleman sat quietly for a moment or two, adjusted his glasses, leaned over towards her and whispered, "Is that one word or two?"

***

A woman scanned the guests at a party and spotted an attractive man standing alone. She approached him.

"Hi, my name is Carmen," she told him.

"That's a beautiful name," he replied. "Is it a family name?"

"No," she replied, "I gave it to myself. It reflects the things I enjoy most, cars and men!" She then asked, "What is your name?"

"B. J. Titsenbeer," he said.

***

There was this businessman who met a beautiful girl and agreed to spend the afternoon with her for five hundred pounds. They went back to her place and did their thing, and before he left, he told her that he did not have any cash on him, but he would have his secretary write a cheque and drop it in the post to her, calling the payment 'Rent for Apartment.'

On the way to the office, he regretted what he had done, realizing that the whole event had not been worth the price. So he had his secretary send a cheque for two hundred and fifty pounds and enclose the following typed note:

Dear Madam

Enclosed find cheque for £250 for rent for your apartment. I am not sending the amount agreed upon, because when I rented the place, I was under the impression that:

It had never been occupied.

There was plenty of heat

It was small enough to make me feel cosy and at home.

However, I found out that it had been previously occupied, that there wasn't any heat, and that it was entirely too large!

Upon receipt of the note, the girl immediately returned the cheque for two hundred and fifty pounds with the following note:

Dear Sir

First, I cannot understand how you could expect a beautiful apartment to remain unoccupied indefinitely. As for the heat, there is plenty of it, if you know how to turn it on!
Regarding the space, the apartment is indeed of regular size, but if you don't have enough furniture to fill it, please do not blame the management.

Please send the rent in full or we will be forced to contact your present Landlady!

***

GREAT TRUTHS THAT LITTLE CHILDREN HAVE LEARNED

1. No matter how hard you try, you can't baptize cats.

2. When your Mum is mad at your Dad, don't let her brush your hair.

3. If your sister hits you, don't hit her back. They always catch the second person.

4. Never ask your three year old brother to hold a tomato.

5. You can't trust dogs to watch your food.

6. Don't sneeze when someone is cutting your hair.

7. Never hold a Dust-Buster and a cat at the same time.

8. You can't hide a piece of broccoli in a glass of milk.

9. Don't wear polka-dot underwear under white shorts.

10. The best place to be when you're sad is Grandpa's lap.

GREAT TRUTHS THAT ADULTS HAVE LEARNED

1. Raising teenagers is like nailing jelly to a tree.

2. Wrinkles don't hurt.

3. Families are like fudge, mostly sweet, with a few nuts.

4. Today's mighty Oak is just yesterday's nut that held its ground.

5. Laughing is a good exercise. It's like jogging on the inside.

6. Middle age is when you choose your cereal for the fibre, not the toy.

GREAT TRUTHS ABOUT GROWING OLD

1. Growing old is mandatory, growing up is optional.

2. Forget the health food. You need all the preservatives you can get.

3. When you fall down, you wonder what else you can do while you are down there.

4. You're getting old when you get the same sensation in a rocking chair you once got from a roller coaster.

5. It's frustrating when you know all the answers, but nobody bothers to ask you the questions.

6. Time might be a great healer, but it is a lousy beautician.

7. Wisdom comes with age, but sometime age comes alone.

THE FOUR STAGES OF LIFE

You believe in Santa Claus.

You don't believe in Santa Claus.

You are Santa Claus.

You look like Santa Claus.

***

SUCCESS

At age 4, success is...not peeing in your pants.

At age 12, success is...having friends.

At age 17, success is...having a driver's licence.

At age 35, success is...having money.

At age 50, success is...having money.

At age 70, success is...having a driver's licence.

At age 80, success is...not peeing in your pants.

DECISIONS, DECISIONS

A man wanted to get married, but he was having trouble choosing from three likely candidates.

So he gives each woman a present of five thousand pounds, and watches to see what they do with the money.

The first does a total makeover. She goes to a fancy beauty salon, gets her hair done, new make up and buys several new outfits and dresses up very nicely for the man. She tells him that she has done this, to be more attractive for him, because she loves him so much!

The man was impressed.

The second woman goes shopping to buy the man gifts. She gets him a new set of golf clubs, some new gizmos for his computer, and some expensive clothes. As she presents these gifts, she tells him that she has spent all the money on him, because she loves him so much!

Again, the man was impressed.

The last candidate invests the money in the stock market. She earns several times the initial five thousand given. She gives him back his five thousand pounds and reinvests the remainder in a joint account. She tells him, that she wants to save for their future, because she loves him so much!

Obviously, the man was suitably impressed.

The man thought for a long time about each of the women, and what they had done, with the money he had given them.

He made his mind up, and married the one with the biggest boobs.

Men are like that, you know!

***

There is more money being spent on breast implants and Viagra today than on research into Alzheimer's. This means that by the year 2040, there should be a large elderly population with perky boobs and huge erections and absolutely no recollection of what to do with them!

***

JUST BE CONTENT WITH HOW THINGS ARE!

A man was sick and tired of going to work every day while his wife stayed at home. He wanted her to see what he went through so he prayed. His prayer went something like this:

> "Dear Lord, I go to work every day and put in eight hours while my wife merely stays at home. I want her to know what I go through! So, please allow her body to switch with mine for a day. Amen!"

God, in his infinite wisdom, granted the man's wish.

Sure enough, the next morning, the man awoke as a woman. He arose, cooked breakfast for his mate, awakened the kids, set out their school clothes, fed them breakfast, packed their lunches, and drove them to school, after which he came home and picked up the dry cleaning, and took it to the cleaners.

After the cleaners, he stopped off at the bank to pay in some money, went to the supermarket to pick up a few items, and then drove home.

When he got home, he made himself a cup of tea, sat down at his computer, went on line and paid some bills, after which he cleaned out the cat's litter box and then bathed the dog!

By now it was 1:00 p.m., so he quickly went upstairs, hurriedly made the beds, collected the laundry basket, vacuumed and dusted all the rooms, then went back down to the kitchen where he loaded and started the washing machine, and mopped the floor.

He then drove to school, to collect the children, and got into an argument with them on the way home. Once home, gave them a milkshake and biscuits and settled them down to do their homework.

He then set up the ironing board and watched TV whilst doing the ironing.

At 4:30 p.m., he began peeling potatoes, washed the vegetables and prepared the pork chops for their evening meal.

After dinner, he loaded the dishes into the dishwasher and started a wash cycle, folded the laundry, bathed the children and put them to bed.

It was now 9:00 p.m.

He was exhausted and, though his daily chores weren't finished, he went to bed where he was expected to make love, which he managed to get through without complaint!

The next morning, he awoke and immediately knelt by the bed and said:

> "Lord, I just do not know what I must have been thinking. I was so wrong to envy my wife's day. Please, Oh! Oh! Please, let us trade back. Amen!"

The lord, in his infinite wisdom, replied:

> "My son, I feel you have learned your lesson, and I will be only too happy to change things back to the way they were. You'll just have to wait for nine months, though. You got pregnant last night!"

PROOF OF WHAT CAN HAPPEN IF A WIFE/GIRLFRIEND DRAGS THEIR PARTNER ALONG SHOPPING

This letter was recently sent by the Head Office of a large national supermarket chain, to a customer in the Oxford area.

Dear Mrs Murray,

While we value your custom and the use of our loyalty card scheme, the manager of your local store, is considering banning you and your family from shopping with us, unless your husband stops his antics.

Below, is a list of offences over the past few months, all of which have been verified by our surveillance cameras.

June 15. Took 24 boxes of condoms and randomly put them in people's trolleys when they weren't looking.

July 2. Set all the alarm clocks in House wares to go off at 5 minute intervals.

July 7. Made a trail of tomato juice on the floor leading to feminine products aisle.

July 19. Walked up to an employee and told her in an official tone, "Code 3 in house wares" and watched what happened.

August 14. Moved a 'Caution-Wet Floor' sign to a carpeted area.

September 15. Set up a tent in the outdoor clothing department and told shoppers he'd invite them in if they would bring sausages and a camping gas stove.

September 23. When the deputy manager asked if she could help him, he began to cry and asked, "Why can't you people just leave me alone?"

October 4. Looked right into the security camera, used it as a mirror, picked his nose and ate it.

November 10. While appearing to be choosing kitchen knives in the house wares aisle, he asked an assistant if he knew where the anti-depressants were.

December 3. Darted around the store suspiciously, loudly humming the 'Mission Impossible' theme tune.

December 6. In the kitchenware aisle, practiced the Madonna look, using different size funnels.

December 18. Hid in a clothing rack and when people browsed, yelled "Pick me! Pick me!"

December 21. When an announcement came over the store tannoy system, assumed the fetal position and screamed, "No! No! It's those voices again!"

December 23. Went into a fitting room, shut the door, waited a while, then yelled, very loudly, "There is no toilet paper in here!"

Yours sincerely

Charles Brown
Customer Relations Manager.

THIS NEXT ONE IS AN EXTRACT FROM
AN AMERICAN NEWSPAPER

A Minneapolis couple decided to go to Florida to thaw out during a particularly icy winter. They planned to stay at the same hotel where they had spent their honeymoon some twenty years earlier.

Because of hectic schedules, the husband left Minnesota and flew to Florida on Thursday, with his wife flying down the following day.

The husband checked into the hotel. There was a computer in his room, so he decided to send an e-mail to his wife. However, he accidentally left out one letter in her e-mail address, and without realizing his error, sent the e-mail.

Meanwhile, somewhere in Houston, a widow had just returned home from her husband's funeral, who was a minister who had had a heart attack and died.

The widow decided to check her e-mail, expecting messages from friends and relatives. After reading the first message, she screamed and fainted.

The widow's son rushed into the room and saw the computer screen which read:

To: My Loving Wife

Subject: I've arrived

Date: October 16, 2004

I know you're surprised to hear from me. They have computers here now and you are allowed to send e-mails to your loved ones. I've just arrived and have been checked in. I see that everything has been prepared for your arrival tomorrow. Looking forward to seeing you then! Hope your journey is as uneventful as mine was.

P.S. Sure is freaking hot down here!

***

A woman meets a man in a bar.

They talk, they connect (there is definitely some chemistry going on here), and end up leaving together.

They get back to his apartment.

As he shows her around, she notices that one wall of his bedroom is completely filled with soft, sweet cuddly teddy bears, arranged on three shelves.

Just hundreds upon hundreds of cute cuddly teddy bears, carefully placed in rows, covering the entire wall!

The woman was touched by the amount of thought he had obviously put into the display.

There were small bears all along the bottom shelf, medium sized bears covered the middle shelf, and huge enormous bears filed the entire top shelf.

She did find it kind of strange for such a masculine guy to have such a large collection of teddy bears. However, she is quite impressed by his sensitive side, and decides not to say anything to him.

They share a bottle of wine and continue talking, and after a while finds herself thinking, *Oh my God! This guy could be the one! Maybe he could be the future father of my children?*

She turns to him and kisses him lightly on the lips, to which he warmly responds.

They continue to kiss, the passion builds, and he romantically lifts her in his arms and caries her through to his bedroom, where they rip off each other's clothes and make hot steamy love.

She is so overwhelmed that she responds with more passion, more creativity, more heat than she has ever known.

After an intense, explosive night of raw passion, they lay together in the afterglow.

The woman rolls over, gently strokes his chest and asks coyly, "Well, how was it?"

The man gently smiles at her, strokes her cheek, looks deeply into her eyes, and says,

"Help yourself to any prize from the middle shelf."

***

TWENTY WAYS TO MAINTAIN A HEALTHY LEVEL
OF INSANITY

At lunchtime, sit in your parked car, wearing a pair of sunglasses, point a hair dryer at passing cars. See if they slow down.

Page yourself over the intercom. Don't disguise your voice.

Every time someone asks you to do something, ask if they want fries with that.

Put your rubbish bin on your desk and label it "IN."

Put decaf in the coffee maker for three weeks. Once everyone has got over their caffeine addictions, switch to Espresso.

On all of the stubs in your cheque book write 'For Smuggling Diamonds.'

Finish all of your sentences with "In accordance with the prophecy."

Don't use any punctuation.

As often as possible, skip rather than walk.

Order a diet water whenever you go out to eat, keeping a serious face.

Specify that your drive through order is to take away.

Sing along at the opera.

Go to a poetry recital and ask why the poems don't rhyme.

Put mosquito netting around your work area and play tropical sounds all day.

Five days in advance, tell your friends that you can't attend their party, because you're not in the mood!

Have your colleagues address you by your wrestling name, "Rock Bottom."

When the money comes out of the cash dispenser, shout out at the top of your voice, "I won! I won!"

When leaving the zoo, start running towards the car park, yelling, "Run for your lives! They're loose!"

Tell your children over dinner, "Due to the economy, we are going to have to let one of you go!"

Finally, the way to keep a healthy level of insanity is to repeat the above to the person nearest to you to make them smile.

***

PRIMARY SCHOOL CHILDREN WRITING
ABOUT THE SEA

This a picture of an octopus. It has eight testicles. (Kelly, age 6)

Oysters balls are called pearls. (James, age 6)

If you are surrounded by sea, you are an island. If you don't have any sea all round you, you are incontinent. (Wayne, age 7)

Sharks are ugly and mean, and have big teeth, just like Emily Richardson. She's not my friend no more. (Kylie, age 6)

A dolphin breathes through an arsehole on the top of its head. (Billy, age 8)

My dad goes out in his boat, and comes back with crabs. (Emily, age 5)

When ships had sails, they used to use the trade winds to cross the oceans. Sometimes, when the wind didn't blow, the sailors would whistle, to make the wind come. My brother said they would have been better off eating beans. (William, age 7)

I like mermaids. They are beautiful, and I like their shiny tails. How do mermaids get pregnant? (Helen, age 6)

I'm not just going to write about the sea. My baby brother is always screaming and being sick. My dad keeps shouting at my mum, and my big sister has just got pregnant, so I can't think what to write. (Amy, age 6)

Some fish are dangerous. Jellyfish can sting, Electric eels can give you a shock. They have to live in caves under the sea where I think they have to plug themselves into chargers. (Christopher, age 7)

When you go swimming in the sea, it is very cold, and it makes my willy small. (Kevin, age 6)

Divers have to be safe when they go under water. Two divers can't go down alone, so they have to go down on each other. (Becky, age 8)

On holiday, my mum went water skiing. She fell off when she was going very fast. She says she won't do it again because water shot up her fanny. (Julie, age 7)

***

A frog goes into a bank and approaches the cashier. He can clearly see from her badge, that her name is Patty Whack.

Miss Whack, I'd like to get a loan for five thousand pounds, to take a holiday.

Patty looks at the frog in disbelief and asks his name.

The frog says his name is Kermit Jagger, his dad is Mick Jagger, and that it's okay, he knows the bank manager.

Patty explains that he will need to secure the loan with some collateral.

Kermit replies, "Sure, no problem, I have this," and produces a tiny porcelain elephant, about an inch tall, bright pink, and perfectly formed.

Very confused, Patty explains that she will have to consult the bank manager, and disappears into a back office.

She finds the manager and says, "There is a frog called Kermit Jagger out there who claims to know you and wants to borrow five thousand pounds, and he wants to use this as collateral," and holds up the tiny pink elephant. "I mean, what in the world is this?"

(You're really going to love this)

The bank manager looks back at her and says, "It's a knickknack, Patty Whack. Give the frog a loan. His old man's a 'Rolling Stone!'"

You've just sang that, haven't you? Yeah, I know you did!

Men Are Just Happier People

NICKNAMES

If Laura, Kate and Sarah go out for lunch, they will call each other by their respective names.

However, if Mike, Dave and John go out, they will affectionately refer to each other as Fat Boy, Godzilla, and Four-eyes.

EATING OUT

When the bill arrives, Mike, Dave and John will each throw in £20, even though it's only for £32.50.

None of them will have anything smaller, and none will actually admit they want change back.

When the girls get their bill, out come the pocket calculators.

MONEY

A man will pay £2 for a £1 item that he needs.

A woman, however, will only pay £1 for a £2 item that she doesn't really need but it's on special offer.

BATHROOMS

A man has six items in his bathroom: Toothbrush, toothpaste, shaving cream, razor, a bar of soap , and a towel from M & S.

The average number of items in the typical women's bathroom is 337.

A man would not be able to identify more than twenty of these items.

ARGUMENTS

A woman has the last word in any argument.

Anything a man says after that is the beginning of a new argument.

CATS

Women love cats.

Men say they love cats, but when women aren't looking, men kick cats.

FUTURE

A woman worries about the future until she gets a husband.

A man never worries about the future until he gets a wife.

SUCCESS

A successful man is one who makes more money than his wife can spend.

A successful woman is one who can find such a man.

MARRIAGE

A woman marries a man expecting he will change, but he doesn't.

A man marries a woman expecting that she won't change, but she does.

DRESSING UP

A woman will dress up to go shopping, water the plants, empty the bins, answer the phones, read a book, and get the post.

A man dresses up for weddings and funerals.

NATURAL

Men wake up as good looking as when they went to bed.

Women somehow deteriorate during the night.

OFFSPRING

Ah, children.

A woman knows all about her children.

She knows about the dentist appointments and romances, best friends, favourite foods, secret fears, hopes and dreams.

A man is vaguely aware of some short people living in the house.

THOUGHT FOR THE DAY

A married man should forget his mistakes.

There's no use in two people remembering the same thing.

***

HEAVEN AND HELL

A Human Resources manager was knocked down, tragically, by a bus and was killed.

Her soul arrived at the pearly gates, where St Peter welcomed her.

"Before you get settled in," he said, "we have never had a Human Resources Manager make it this far before, and we are really not sure what to do with you."

"Oh I see," said the woman. "Can't you just let me in?"

"Well, I'd like to," said St Peter, "but I have higher orders. We are instructed to let you have a day in Heaven and a day in Hell, and then you are to choose where you would like to spend all eternity."

"Actually, I think I would prefer heaven," said the woman.

"Sorry, but we do have rules," at which St Peter put the HR Manager into the downward bound lift.

As the doors opened in Hell, she stepped out onto a beautiful golf course.

In the distance was a country club. Around her were many friends, past fellow executives, all smartly dressed, happy and cheering for her.

They ran up and kissed her on both cheeks, and they talked about old times.

They played a perfect round of golf and afterwards went to the country club where she enjoyed a superb steak and lobster dinner.

She met the Devil (who was actually rather nice) and she had a wonderful night, telling jokes and dancing.

Before she knew it, it was time to leave, everyone shook her hand and waved as she stepped into the elevator.

The elevator took her back up to heaven, where St Peter was waiting for her.

"Now it is time to spend a day in heaven," he said.

So she spent the next twenty four hours lounging around on clouds, playing the harp and singing, which was almost as enjoyable as her day in hell.

At the day's end St Peter returned. "So," he said, "you've spent a day in hell and you've spent a day in heaven. You must choose between the two."

The woman though for a second and replied, "Well. Heaven is certainly lovely, but I actually had a better time in Hell."

Accordingly, St Peter took her to the elevator again and she went back down to Hell.

When the doors of the elevator opened, she found herself standing in a desolate wasteland, covered in rubbish and filth.

She saw her friends dressed in rags, picking up rubbish and putting it in old sacks.

The Devil approached and put his arm around her.

"I don't understand," she stuttered. "Yesterday I was here, and there was a golf course, and a country club. We ate lobster, and we danced and we had a wonderful, happy time. Now all there is, is just a dirty wasteland of rubbish and all my friends look miserable!"

The Devil simply looked at her and smiled, "Yesterday we were recruiting you, today you're staff!"

***

WHY I FIRED MY SECRETARY

Last week was my birthday, and I did not feel very well when I woke up on that morning.

I went down the stairs to breakfast, hoping my wife would be pleasant and say, "Happy Birthday!" and possibly have a small present for me.

As it turned out, she barely said "good morning," let alone "Happy Birthday."

I thought, well that's marriage for you, but the kids, they will remember!

The children came bounding downstairs to breakfast and did not say a word.

So when I left for the office, I felt pretty low and somewhat despondent.

As I walked into my office, my secretary Jane said, "Good Morning, Boss, and by the way, Happy Birthday!"

It felt a little better that at least someone had remembered.

I worked until one o'clock, when Jane knocked on my door and said, "You know, it's such a beautiful day outside, and it is your birthday, what do you say we go out to lunch, just you and me."

I said, "Thanks, Jane, that's the greatest thing I've heard all day. Let's go!"

We went to lunch, but we did not go where normally we would go. She chose instead a quiet bistro with a private table. We had two Martinis each, and thoroughly enjoyed the meal.

On the way back to the office, Jane said, "You know, it's such a beautiful day! We don't have to go straight back to the office, do we?"

I responded, "I guess not. What do you have in mind?"

She replied, "Let's drop by my apartment, it's just round the corner."

After arriving at her apartment, Jane turned to me and said, "Boss, if you don't mind, I'm just going to step into the bedroom for just a moment. I'll be right back."

"Okay," I nervously replied.

She went into the bedroom and, after a couple of minutes, she came out carrying a huge birthday cake, followed by my wife, my children, and dozens of my friends and colleagues, all singing "Happy Birthday."

I just sat there, on the couch, STARK NAKED.

NOBODY'S PERFECT!

There was this woman, who had to go into hospital for minor surgery.

The day came for her to be admitted and go under the surgeon's knife.

During what should have been a routine op, complications set in. She travels down that tunnel of brilliant white light, and when she reaches the far end, God is there waiting for her.

"Oops," said God, "I've made a bit of a mistake, you're not who I thought it was. You're not due here for another thirty-nine years, seven months, eleven days, eighteen hours, twenty three minutes and ten seconds!" and promptly sends her back through the tunnel, on to the operating table.

The surgeon and his medical support team all congratulate one another on bringing the woman back to life, and successfully complete the surgery.

Whilst the woman was recovering from her ordeal in her private room in hospital, it all started to come back to her, the brilliant white light, God's voice, and the words he had said to her. She decided there and then, that as she had over thirty nine years left on this planet, she was going to treat herself to the full works.

After a couple of days, she was discharged and sent home, where she set to work straight away, making appointments to see famous Harley Street plastic surgeons, dental surgeons, together with top hair stylists and makeup artists to the stars!

Once again the day came, she was admitted to the clinic of the plastic surgeon, where she underwent a full facial, liposuction, in fact you name it, she had it done.

Several days later, after the swelling and bruising had started to go down, she was discharged and allowed to go home.

The following month, she visited the dentist's surgery on a couple of occasions, where she underwent various stages of treatment to straighten and whiten her teeth, to give her the perfect smile.

After a couple of months, all was ready, she just needed her hair to be worked on and a makeover on her face and she was finished.

That time came, she had had all of the plastic surgery completed, the dental treatment, the hair was of the latest style, and her makeup was perfect.

She walked out of the beauty salon onto the busy high street, stepped off of the pavement and was hit by a No. 39 bus. Did not stand a chance, she died instantly.

For the second time in a year, she finds herself travelling down that tunnel of bright white light and, sure enough, God is waiting for her.

She said, "God, I thought you said I had over thirty nine years of my life left when we last met!"

"Oops," said God, "I'm awfully sorry, seems like I've dropped another clanger, because you have changed the way you look, I did not recognise you!"

***

With this next one, I am sure we have all been there at some time or other in our lives. But please read on, and by the end I'm sure many of you will be saying to yourselves, "Boy, I wish I'd written that!"

PASSPORT APPLICATION LETTER

Dear Minister,

I'm in the process of renewing my passport but I am at a total loss to understand or believe the hoops I am being asked to jump through.

How is it that Bert Smith of TV Rentals Basingstoke has my address and telephone number and knows that I bought a satellite dish from them back in 1994, and yet, the government is still asking me where I was born and on what date?

How come that nice West African immigrant chappy who comes round every Thursday night with his DVD rental's van can tell me every film or video I have had out since he started his business up eleven years ago, yet you still want me to remind you of my last three jobs, two of which were with contractors working for the government?

How come the TV detector van can tell if my TV is on, what channel I am watching and whether I have paid my licence or not, and yet if I win the government run lottery they have no idea I have won or where I am and will keep the bloody money to themselves if I fail to claim in good time.

Do you people do this by hand?

You have my date of birth on numerous files that you hold on me, including the one with all the income tax forms I've filed for the past thirty odd years. It's on my health insurance card, my driver's licence, on the last four passports I've had, on all those stupid customs declaration forms I've had to fill out before being allowed off the planes and boats over the last thirty years, and all those insufferable census forms that are done every ten years and the electoral registration forms I have to complete by law, every time our lords and masters are up for re-election.

Would somebody please take note, once and for all, I was born in Maidenhead on the 4th March 1957, my mother's name is Mary, her maiden name was Reynolds, my father's name is Robert, and I'd be absolutely astounded if that ever changed between now and the day I die!

I apologise, Minister. I'm obviously not myself this morning. But between you and me, I have simply had enough! You mail the application to my house, then you ask me for my address. What is going on? Do you have a gang of Neanderthals working there? Look at my damn picture. Do I look like Bin Laden? I do not want to activate the Fifth Reich for God's sake! I just want to go and park my weary backside on a sunny, sandy beach for a couple of weeks' well earned rest away from all this crap!

Well, I have to go now, because I have to go back to Salisbury and get another copy of my birth certificate because you lost the last one, and to the tune of sixty quid! What a racket that is! Would it be so complicated to have all the services in the same building, to assist in the issuance of a new passport the same day? But oooh noooo, that'd be too damn easy and make sense. You'd rather have us running all over the place like headless chickens, then find some tosser to confirm that it's really me in the picture, you know, the one where we're not allowed to smile in, in case we look as if we are enjoying the process.

Hey, you know why we can't smile? Cos we're totally jacked off!

I served in the armed forces for more than twenty-five years, including ten years at the Ministry of defence in London. I have had security clearances which allowed me to sit in the Cabinet office, five seats away from the Prime Minister while he was being briefed on the first Gulf war, and I have been doing volunteer work for the British red Cross ever since I left the services. However, I have to get someone like my doctor, who, before he got his medical degree six months ago, was LIVING IN PAKISTAN!

Yours sincerely,

An Irate British Citizen

***

THE CASH MACHINE

Please follow the appropriate steps for your gender.

MALE PROCEDURE

Drive up to the cash machine.

Wind down your window.

Insert card into machine and enter PIN.

Enter amount of cash required and withdraw.

Retrieve card, cash and receipt.

Wind window back up.

Drive off.

FEMALE PROCEDURE

Drive up to the cash machine.

Reverse the required amount to align window with machine.

Apply hand brake, wind window down.

Find handbag, empty contents onto the passenger seat to locate card.

Tell person on mobile phone that you will call back, and hang up.

Attempt to insert card into machine.

Open card door to allow easier access to machine due to its excessive distance from the car.

Insert card.

Re-insert card the correct way.

Trawl through contents of handbag on passenger seat for diary with PIN number written inside.

Enter PIN.

Press cancel and re-enter correct PIN.

Enter amount of cash required.

Check makeup in rear view mirror.

Retrieve cash and receipt.

Place cash inside wallet and stuff everything on passenger seat back into handbag.

Write debit amount on cheque stub and place cheque book and receipt in handbag.

Re-check makeup.

Close door, wind window back up and drive forward two feet.

Reverse back two feet to cash machine.

Open door and retrieve card.

Re-empty handbag, locate card wallet, and place card in empty pocket in wallet.

Give dirty look to irate male driver waiting behind you.

Close door, restart engine and drive off.

Redial person on mobile phone.

Drive for two to three miles.

Release hand brake.

***

RUDE CUSTOMER

This next story is for all employees who work with rude customers. An award should certainly go to the Virgin Airlines gate attendant in Sydney, some time ago, for being smart and funny while making her point, when confronted with a passenger who probably deserved to fly as cargo.

A crowded Virgin flight was cancelled, after the company's 767s had been withdrawn from service. A single attendant was re-booking a long queue of inconvenienced travellers. Suddenly, an angry passenger pushed his way to the desk. He slapped his ticket down on the counter and said, "I HAVE to be on this flight and it HAS to be first class!"

The attendant calmly replied, "I'm sorry, sir. I'll be happy to try to help you, but I've got to help these people first, and I'm sure we'll be able to work something out."

The passenger was unimpressed. He asked loudly, so that the passengers behind him could hear, "DO YOU HAVE ANY IDEA WHO I AM?"

Without hesitating, the attendant smiled, grabbed her public address microphone: "May I have your attention please, may I have your attention please," she began, her voice heard clearly throughout the terminal, "We have a passenger here at gate 14 WHO DOES NOT KNOW WHO HE IS. If anyone can help him find his identity, please come to gate 14."

With the people in the queue behind him laughing hysterically, the man glared at the attendant, gritted his teeth and said, "F*** you!"

Without flinching, she smiled and said, "I'm sorry, sir, but you'll have to get in line for that, too!"

GOLF

Four lawyers in a law firm lived and died for their Saturday morning round of golf. It was their favourite time of the week.

Then one of the lawyers was transferred to an office in another city. It wasn't quite the same without him.

A new woman lawyer joined their law firm. One day she overheard the remaining three talking about their golf round at the coffee table.

Curious, she spoke up, "You know, I used to play on my golf team in college and I was pretty good. Would you mind if I joined you next week?"

The three lawyers looked at each other. They were hesitant. Not one of them wanted to say yes, but she had them on the spot. Finally, one of them said it would be ok, but they would be starting pretty early, at 6:30 a.m. He figured the early tee-time would discourage her immediately.

The woman said this might be a problem and asked if she could possibly be up to fifteen minutes late. They rolled their eyes but said this would be ok. She smiled and said, "Good, then I'll be there either at 6:30 a.m. or 6:45."

She showed up right on 6:30 and wound up beating all three of them, with an eye opening 2-under par round. She was a fun and pleasant person, the entire round. The men were impressed!

The next week, she again showed up at 6:30 on the Saturday morning. Only this time she played left-handed. The three lawyers were incredulous as she still managed to beat them with an even par round, despite playing with her off round. By now, they were totally amazed, but wondered if she was just trying to make them look bad by beating them left-handed. They just could not figure her out.

In the third week, they all had their game faces on. But this week, she was fifteen minutes late! This had the men irritable, because each was determined to play the best round of golf in his life to beat her.

As they waited for her, they figured her late arrival was some petty gamesmanship on her part. Finally she showed up. This week the lady lawyer played right-handed, which was a good thing, since she narrowly beat all three of them.

Back in the clubhouse, she had all three of them shaking their heads at her ability.

Finally, one of the men could contain his curiosity no longer. He asked her point-blank, "How do you decide if you're going to play left or right-handed?"

The lady lawyer blushed and grinned. She said, "That's easy. When my dad taught me to play golf, I learned I was ambidextrous. I have always had fun switching back and forth. Then when I met my husband in college and got married, I discovered he always sleeps in the nude. From then on I developed a silly habit. Right before I left in the morning for golf practice, I would pull the covers off him. If his you-know-what was pointing to the right, I golfed right-handed and if it pointed to the left, I golfed left-handed. All the girls on the team thought this was hysterical."

Astonished at this bizarre explanation, one of the men shot back, "But what if it's pointed straight up in the air?"

She replied, "Simple, I'm fifteen minutes late!"

***

Question: What is an Australian kiss?

Answer: It's the same as a French kiss, only "down under."

Question: What do you do with 365 used condoms?

Answer: Melt them down, make a tyre, and call it a Goodyear!

Question: Why are hurricanes normally named after women?

Answer: Because when they come, they're wild and wet. But when they go, they take your house and your car with them.

Question: Why do girls rub their eyes when they get up in the morning?

Answer: Because they don't have any balls to scratch!

***

WILL SOMEBODY PLEASE LOCK ME UP!

IN PRISON	IN WORK
You get three meals a day, fully paid.	You get a break for one meal a day, and you have to pay for it.

IN PRISON	IN WORK
For good behaviour, you get time off.	For good behaviour, you get more work.

IN PRISON	IN WORK
The warden locks and unlocks all the doors for you.	You must carry a security card and open all the doors yourself.

IN PRISON	IN WORK
You can watch TV and play games.	You could get fired for watching TV and playing games.

IN PRISON	IN WORK
You get your own toilet.	You have to share the toilet with people who pee on the seat.

IN PRISON	IN WORK
They allow your family and friends to visit.	You aren't even supposed to speak to your family.

IN PRISON	IN WORK
All expenses are paid for by the taxpayers, with no work required.	You must pay all your expenses to go to work, and they deduct taxes from your salary to pay for prisoners.

IN PRISON	IN WORK
You spend most of your life inside bars, wanting to get out.	You spend most of your time wanting to get out to go inside bars.

IN PRISON	IN WORK
You must deal with sadistic wardens	They are called 'managers.'

***

Christian Ronaldo, the famous Manchester United & Portuguese International footballer, when quizzed about the break up of his relationship with his fiancé, simply replied that he found it difficult to be in a relationship with someone better looking than himself, so he decided to finish it.

A couple of days later, Ronaldo's ex decided to issue her own version of the breakup, to the media, stating that she found it impossible to have a relationship with him, on the grounds that whenever she got close up to him, he would fall over!

***

COMPILATION OF EXCERPTS FROM RADIO AND TV QUIZ PROGRAMMES

Quizmaster: "What is another name for 'cherrypickers' and 'cheesemongers?'"

Contestant: "Homosexuals?"

Quizmaster: "No, they're regiments in the British Army, who will be very upset with you."

***

Quizmaster: "Where do you think Cambridge University is?"

Contestant: "Geography isn't my strong point."

Quizmaster: "There's a clue in the title."

Contestant: "Leicester."

***

Quizmaster: "Who had a worldwide hit with 'What a Wonderful World?'"

Contestant: "I don't know."

Quizmaster: "I'll give you some clues: What do you call the part between your hand and your elbow?"

Contestant: "Arm."

163

Quizmaster: "Correct, and if you're not weak, you're...?"

Contestant: "Strong."

Quizmaster: "Correct, and what was Lord Mountbatten's first name?"

Contestant: "Louis."

Quizmaster: "Well, there we are then. So who had a worldwide hit with the song 'What a Wonderful World?'"

Contestant: "Was it Frank Sinatra?"

***

Quizmaster: "What is the capital of Italy?"

Contestant: "France."

Quizmaster: "France is another country, have another try."

Contestant: "Oh, er, em, Benidorm."

Quizmaster: "Wrong, sorry, let's try another question. In which country is the Pantheon?"

Contestant: "Sorry, I don't know."

Quizmaster: "Just take a guess then."

Contestant: "Paris."

***

Quizmaster: "Oscar Wilde, Adolf Hitler and Jeffrey Archer have all written books about their experiences in what: Prison or the Conservative party?"

Contestant: "The conservative party."

***

Quizmaster: "For ten pounds, what is the nationality of the Pope?"

Contestant: "I think I know that one. Is it Jewish?"

***

Quizmaster: "What was Ghandi's first name?"

Contestant: "Goosey?"

***

Quizmaster: "What happened in Dallas on November 22, 1963?"

Contestant: "I don't know, I wasn't watching it then."

***

Quizmaster: "What is the name of the long running TV comedy show about pensioners: 'Last of the...?' "

Contestant: "Mohicans."

***

Quizmaster: "What is eleven squared?"

Contestant: "I don't know."

Quizmaster: "I'll give you a clue. It's two ones, with a two in the middle."

Contestant: "Is it five?"

***

Quizmaster: "Which American actor is married to Nicole Kidman?"

Contestant: "Forrest Gump."

***

Quizmaster: "On which street did Sherlock Holmes live?"

Contestant: "Erm..."

Quizmaster: "He makes bread…"

Contestant: "Umm…"

Quizmaster: "He makes cakes."

Contestant: "Kipling Street."

***

Quizmaster: "Which is the largest Spanish speaking country in the world?"

Contestant: "Barcelona."

Quizmaster: "I was really looking for the name of the country."

Contestant: "I'm sorry, I don't know the names of many countries in Spain."

***

Quizmaster: "What is the world's largest continent?"

Contestant: "The Pacific."

***

Quizmaster: "Name a film starring Bob Hoskins that is also the name of a famous painting by Leonardo Da Vinci."

Contestant: "Who framed Roger Rabbit?"

***

Quizmaster: "What was signed to bring World War One to an end in 1918?"

Contestant: "Was it the Magna Carta?"

***

Quizmaster: "How many kings of England have been called Henry?"

Contestant: "Er, well, I know there was a Henry the Eighth, er... er... Three?

***

Quizmaster: "In which European country is Mount Etna?"

Contestant: "Japan."

Quizmaster: "I did say in which European country, so in case you didn't hear that, I can let you try again."

Contestant: "Er... Mexico?"

***

Quizmaster: "How long did the six day war between Egypt and Israel last?"

Contestant: (After a long pause) "Fourteen days."

***

Quizmaster: "In which country would you spend shekels?"

Contestant: "Holland?"

Quizmaster: "Try the next letter of the alphabet."

Contestant: "Iceland? Ireland?"

Quizmaster: "It's a bad line. Did you say Israel?"

Contestant: "No."

***

Quizmaster: "What 'K' could be described as the Islamic Bible?"

Contestant: "Er…"

Quizmaster: "It's got two syllables… Kor…"

Contestant: "Blimey?"

Quizmaster: "Ha ha ha, no. The past participle of run."

Contestant: (absolute silence)

Quizmaster: "Okay, try it another way. Today I run, yesterday I..."

Contestant: "Walked?"

***

Quizmaster: "What is the name given to the condition where the sufferer can fall asleep at any time?"

Contestant: "Nostalgia?"

***

Quizmaster: "What religion was Guy Fawkes?"

Contestant: "Jewish?"

Quizmaster: "That's close enough!"

***

Quizmaster: "Johnny Weissmuller died on this day. Which jungle-swinging character, clad only in a loin cloth, did he play?"

Contestant: "Jesus?"

***

THE HOLIDAY – YOU JUST DON'T KNOW WHO YOU MIGHT BUMP INTO!

Two priests decided that they would go to Hawaii on holiday.

They were determined to make this a real holiday by not wearing anything that would identify them as being clergy.

As soon as their plane landed, they headed straight for the nearest store, and bought themselves some really outrageous shorts, shirts sandals and sunglasses, etc.

The very next morning, they went off to the beach, dressed in their 'tourist' garb.

They were laying on sunbeds, enjoying a drink, the sunshine, and taking in the scenery, when a "drop dead gorgeous" blonde, wearing only the bottom part of a bikini, came walking straight towards them. As you could imagine, they couldn't help but stare at her.

As the blond walked past, she smiled and nodded to them both and said, "Good Morning Father, Good Morning Father," addressing them each individually, then she passed on by.

They were both stunned.

How in the world, did she know that they were both priests?

So the next day, they went back to the store that they visited on their arrival, and bought even more outrageous outfits.

The shirts and shorts were so loud, you could hear them before you saw them!

Once again, in their new attire, they went to the beach, and settled down on their sunbeds, sipped at their drinks and enjoyed the sunshine.

After a little while, the same gorgeous blonde, wearing a different bikini bottom, taking her sweet time, came walking towards them.

Again she nodded at each of them, saying, "Good Morning, Father, Good Morning, Father," and started to walk away.

One of the priests could stand it no longer and said, "Just a minute, young lady."

"Yes father?"

"We are priests and proud of it, but I have to know, how in the world do you know we are priests, dressed as we are?"

"Father, it's me, Sister Kathleen," was her reply!

***

A man is getting into the shower, just as his wife is finishing hers, when the doorbell rings. The wife quickly wraps herself in her towel and runs downstairs. When she opens the door, there stands Bob, their next door neighbour. Before she can say a word, Bob says, "I'll give you £800 to drop that towel." After thinking for a moment, she drops her towel, and stands naked in front of Bob. After a few seconds, Bob, true to his word, hands her the £800 and leaves. The woman wraps herself back up in the towel and goes back upstairs. As she walks into the bathroom, her husband asks, "Who was that?"

"It was Bob, our neighbour," she replies.

"Great!" says the husband, "Did he mention anything about the £800 he owes me?"

***

Lightning Source UK Ltd.
Milton Keynes UK
29 November 2010

163614UK00003B/40/P